Children's Time in Worship

Children's Time in Worship

ARLINE J. BAN

Judson Press® Valley Forge

CHILDREN'S TIME IN WORSHIP

Copyright © 1981
Judson Press, Valley Forge, PA 19481

Library of Congress Cataloging in Publication Data
Ban, Arline J.
  Children's time in worship.
  Includes index.
  1. Worship (Religious education) I. Title.
BV1522.B266   264'.0088054   81-11805
ISBN 0-8170-0902-7   AACR2

The name JUDSON PRESS is registered as a trademark in the U.S. Patent Office.
Printed in the U.S.A. ⊕

Foreword

"Children should be seen and not heard" is one way churches have perceived the presence of children. Translated into practical terms, this meant children should not be children with needs and voices of their own. And in terms of church programs, adult planners were relieved of the need to provide more helpfully for children related to their church.

Fortunately such blind perceptions have been changing, and more of us, at all ages, are hearing what Jesus meant when he rebuked those who stood in the way of his relationship to children. Before a church is able to obey the imperative of Jesus, who said, "Let the children come . . .," the church must understand and find ways to "let the children *be.*" *Being* is necessary to coming and, indeed, to *becoming.*

For this reason I am pleased to introduce this book by Arline Ban. She helps us to see that worship needs its own integrity but that children need integrity also. We need to accept their feelings, emotions, thoughts, and imagination, together with the other realities that pertain to their age and attention span. Arline helps us to know that children are not miniature adults and that to respect their need for space and personal involvement will bring about changes in the way a church plans to meet their essential feeling needs so that children are not suffered as "silent observers" but as vocal participants. The suggestions in this book are not only related to real churches but also to real children whose world is very real to them. Just as we have heard that "tokenism" is not a solution to racism or sexism, we can all profit from learning that tokenism directed toward children fails to satisfy their needs. Most important, it fails to take Jesus seriously. He refused to postpone relationships with children until they had learned how to behave or until they were more mature! Children are teachable. I invite you to let them teach you through the insights of this book.

—William F. Keucher, Pastor,
The Covenant Baptist Church,
West Bloomfield, Michigan
President, 1980-1981,
American Baptist Churches in the U.S.A.,
Valley Forge, Pennsylvania

Contents

Chapter 1

Children in the Worship of the Church

Consider the Children

The flowers are in place . . . .
Ushers pass out the bulletins . . . .
The music prelude begins . . . .
Enter the minister and choir to take their places . . . .
Scampering down the aisle come the lively children.
Riding high on the shoulders of parents come the thumb-sucking babes.
Why do they come? we ask.
Why break the peaceful solitude of the sanctuary?
What right do they have to intrude upon worship?
Why are children allowed to be in the worship of the church?

This book explores some possibilities for sharing with children in corporate worship. We will look at ways to make these special moments with children creative and meaningful for all who gather to worship. In order to do this we need to appreciate the place of children in the worshiping community.

The Place of the Child in Corporate Worship

The Gospel accounts remind us of the importance of the child in our midst. Jesus was angry when his disciples turned the children away. He not only recognized their value, but he also acted out what he said by involving them in the gathering. ". . . he took the children in his arms, placed his hands on each of them, and blessed them" (Mark 10:16, TEV). This incident also calls attention to the importance of a "childlike faith." Children need to participate along with the worshiping community; we adults as well need them to remind us of a joyful spirit as we respond to God in life.

Historically speaking, the Christian church has not always included children in the active life of the church. The traditions, structures, and language have allowed them little room. The liturgy and celebration of the sacraments have been reserved for adult understanding and response. In many communions children have been entirely excluded from corporate worship until they reach the stage at which personal commitment is possible.

This historical pattern is still evident in many of our churches today. Corporate worship is usually adult centered, planned for those who are already a part of the community of believers. Any evangelical purpose to awaken the awareness of God's love is directed exclusively to adult experience. Even though children may be present in the gathering, their role is to observe rather than to take part in worship. More often children are excluded from corporate worship altogether and are delegated to their own age group activity where they may engage in a worship experience on their own level of understanding. It is at this point, however, that we raise the question, Is it always best for the young to be treated separately? Much can be gained from sharing with persons of different ages. Children, as well as youth and adults, can learn from personal relationships and the happenings that take place in intergenerational groups. This also applies to worship. Children may gain Christian values as they experience worship with adults. Christian education, to be adequate, includes teaching children about God and the people of God, as well as enabling them to experience being "one of" the Christian community.

Children need to feel that being a part of the church is like being a part of the family. For example, if a child is isolated—put in another part of the house with a nurse for mealtimes and playtimes until the child grows up—he or she will find it difficult to feel a sense of belonging within the family circle. Separating children can make them feel unimportant to the total fellowship. It is essential that a child have a sense of belonging and experience meaningful relationships within the worshiping community from an early age.

There are those who would include children in worship so that the children might have an "example" of how to act. They want children to see adult models going through the rituals in which the "people of God" engage. Yet examples are ambiguous teachers. The growing individual may discover negative as well as positive meanings in human examples. Indeed, there is even a high risk that persons will rebel against examples. At this point we are reminded that the primary means by which children learn is not through "examples" but through their own experiences. We learn about the people of God at worship by being one of them, by taking part along with the rest of the Christian community.

Children do have a place in the worshiping community. Our concern for their spiritual growth leads us to discover how to enable them to be participants. We want them to share in the experience rather than be observers in an adult-centered worship service. We will try to understand the child's perspective of worship and use that understanding as a guide as we seek to make children a part of corporate worship.

The Child's View of Worship

Children find meaning and understand the faith in different ways according to their own individual growth and unique life experience. Persons of the same age and similar background, however, do have common needs and experiences. They are usually able to interpret life on a similar level of understanding. In our ministry with children we recognize that they learn best when what is happening relates to what they know and experience and when things are explained in a language the children understand. Careful preparation is needed for presence and participation of children in corporate worship. First, a word about the nature of worship.

Corporate worship is celebration. It is the celebration of the Good News in Jesus Christ. It celebrates new life in Christ, liberation of human beings in every phase of life. Worship as celebration enables our awareness of God's activity in the past and God's continued love in our present good and bad times. Worship evokes a response to God's activity from individual persons and the congregation.

Sharing in the act of corporate worship gives persons an opportunity to sense the reality of God and to respond with thinking and feeling to an encounter with God.

It is vital that children have the opportunity to experience worship as part of the larger church fellowship. In corporate worship children may respond with their own feelings as they sense the mystery and depth that is central to the life of the community. They, too, may be guided in their own response to God. We need to keep in mind that the child encounters worship quite differently at various stages of growth.

The Young Child

The young child is "me" centered. The typical world for a

three-year-old is home, parents, pets, and those relationships and events that revolve around each one's life. As the nursery-age child grows in feelings of security and develops trust in the surrounding environment, a natural "moving out" takes place. The child begins to explore other relationships and to prove autonomy in a larger world.

John, a typical three-year-old, was hesitant to leave his mother in the church pew to go to the front with the children. She pushed him out into the aisle. He moved slowly. He looked up at those strange faces peering down at him from either side of the aisle. Then he turned and dashed back to his mother and hid his face in her lap. Six months later John slowly took the hand of an older child and moved forward to join the children. A year later he does not hesitate at all. John feels comfortable with some of those no longer "strange" faces. He recognizes many as friends he met in the supermarket or people he saw at the church suppers. By the time he is five, John's world is rapidly enlarging. He is busy in school or playing at another child's home. He has a vivid imagination and relates to others easily. John thinks the minister and his teachers are special friends. John feels a part of the church family.

Young children like John share the worship service on a feeling level before they are able to understand what is going on or why. Their feelings of security are important. A young child may feel, *I like sitting close to my family. . . . The people like me. . . . I feel good here. . . . They don't mind when I wiggle or drop the paper. . . . People like to sing and pray.*

Children may sense the value adults place on worship as they grow and recognize the feelings of others. They may feel the seriousness of those intentional acts of worship that express adoration, thanksgiving, and confession even though they do not understand the words or depth of expression. Their awareness of God's love comes through people.

The Child in the Early Grades

Each child grows at a different pace, but, generally speaking, children in grades one to three are somewhat alike. They are active and on the go. They seem to sense the growth of their larger muscles, for they are always in motion trying to see how they can jump, skip, run, or bend. They are learning to be independent. On the other hand, they need lots of affection and the attention of adults. They like to perform group activities with their peers. Yet they tend to be bossy, even rigid, when it comes to rules. They can be both clever and hurtful with their teasing. These children are learning to read, to write, and to do simple math. They understand more of the language than they can read. Ideas shared with children of this age must be concrete and real because they understand all things in tangible (perceived by touch) and experienced ways. Younger children are not ready to digest symbolic ideas, but they can make use of the experiences of the Bible. For better communication, stories and incidents from Scripture need to be specific and related to the child's experiences. Concrete experiences, evidenced by the five senses, can be learned, while symbols, ideas, and theological images are best left to the later teen and adult years. For example, sheep will mean something to a farm child who has experienced real live sheep, but they will mean less to the young child in the city who may have had little or no experience with farms or sheep. Keeping language and stories at the experiential, feeling level helps one communicate with younger children. Again, ideas must be concrete and real for them to grasp, for they are literalists.

Janet enters the sanctuary and receives a big hug from her friend the usher. Sitting in the pew with her family, she kicks her foot to her own rhythm until the organist begins to play. Then her whole body is set in motion, picking up the beat of the hymn to be sung. She finds the right page in the hymnbook. Janet joins the singing and is able to read all of the words except "alleluia." She does not recognize it on the page. She sees how happily the people in front are singing, so she joins them. As the people pray the Lord's Prayer, Janet wonders just where heaven is and if God looks like her father or Peter's father. And trespasses! *They must be awful things!* she thinks. But when the minister says, ". . . forgive us . . .," Janet remembers, *I'm glad Mom forgave me when I broke her dish.* As the words are spoken, her mind translates them into images she can see or understand in what she experiences. Symbols, language with abstract meanings, pass over her head.

Janet understands worship on a feeling level as she experiences God's love through péople. The affirmation and love she receives helps her to be aware of the people of God who do love and help one another. Even though she does not know the full meaning of what is going on or how to act, she senses awe and wonder in the beauty of the music and in the surroundings. She is aware of the attitude and the spirit of the leaders and people in the congregation. Janet knows the church includes her as she shares in worship. She is able to listen, even though with limited understanding, to sing songs of praise, and to thank God for the life she knows.

The Older Child

Older elementary children fit into the category of fourth to sixth graders. These children continue to be active, to grow in awareness of other people and a larger world around them. They are becoming more skilled with the use of their bodies and are often involved in competitive sports and games. Friends are important. But at home sibling rivalry often reigns. Older children are discovering that there are many life-styles and value systems in a society made up of different people. They are aware of the need to make choices about what is right or fair or just and sometimes they find the decision making difficult. They may feel parents are okay, at times, that is. However, adults are important as role models, for older children tend to latch on to heroes and heroines. Many older children carry out responsibility well when they feel they are being treated as persons in their own right. They still understand ideas and language in literal, concrete ways, but they are slowly growing into being able to understand abstract symbolic thinking.

The words caught Tim's ear: "I was hungry and you fed me, . . . I was sick and you took care of me. . . ." Tim had heard the words of Jesus before. Sure, he had studied them in the church school. But now there was another familiar ring. The day before, Tim, Mike, Jane, and Becky, "his gang," had gone with their church family group to help Mrs. Peters. They had cleaned her home and yard and filled her cupboard with canned foods and home-baked goods. Mike's mother had called on Mrs. Peters a couple of weeks ago. She had discovered that Mrs. Peters had been in need of help for some time with no one to care for her. Her home was in a mess and there was little food for her to eat. Mike's mother had taken her to the doctor and had helped her while she got better. Then she had asked if their family group might come to straighten up her home. Glad for the attention, Mrs. Peters had said it was all right. It had been a fun day working to help someone else.

Mike felt happy inside. He felt good about the people in his church and how they cared for others. Today in church he heard the Scriptures and the prayers and sang the hymns with more meaning. He was aware of God's presence. Mike responded with thanksgiving and a promise to try to act out the words of Jesus when he could.

Older children respond to the worship experience in many of the same ways younger children do. As they grow, they are able to know much more about the significance of worship. When they observe people praising God and asking for God's help and guidance, they may understand the church as a group of people for whom worship is at the center of their lives. They may identify worship as the source of strength, direction, and support for living out the Christian faith. Older children are beginning to sense their own responsibility for times when they are involved in wrongdoing and unfair treatment, particularly as they grow in awareness of self and of a larger world. They, too, are able to experience worship, to give thanks and pray for help in personal decision making as well as pray for solutions to world problems. These growing young people are also ready to study the traditions, the sacraments, and the rituals of worship and to recognize their significance in Christian commitment.

Children bring what they are and what they understand to corporate worship. We need to consider their abilities and needs as we plan for their participation.

The special time set aside to share with children in the worship service is not the only way children may be involved. Whenever they are present, there is the possibility for awareness and response in the worship experience. As we acknowledge the place of children in corporate worship, we will plan for their involvement.

Involving Children in the Worship Experience

Let us look carefully at what may be happening to children in corporate worship. How are we involving them in the worship celebration as persons and as a part of the community?

Many of us allow the children to sit in to observe the rituals of worship and then ask them to leave without recognition when the service might get too heavy for them or too long for their span of attention. By asking the children to leave, we are getting rid of distractions for the adults. It also gives the children a chance to have a more satisfying experience elsewhere. However, we may well be ignoring children in following this pattern. Without knowing it, we may be communicating to children that they are too young to understand or to have the privileges of sharing in the "real" experience of worship.

On the other hand, we may give only "token" recognition to children in corporate worship. This may happen when we ask children to leave at a certain time during the singing of a hymn or we say a prayer "over" the children. "Token" recognition is given when we call attention to children without really involving them in the feeling, thinking, responsive nature of worship.

Providing a teaching/learning opportunity for children while adults worship is a good plan. It is better than encouraging children to sit quietly through an adult-centered worship service, only to draw pictures of the minister on a bulletin. What they learn from the latter might be to "tune out" what is happening around them, a habit that unfortunately carries over into adulthood. The need is to find ways to involve children meaningfully when they are present in corporate worship.

Through Listening and Responding

It has been suggested that it is possible for children to be caught up in the aesthetic quality of worship. Like others in the worshiping community, their awareness of God's presence will come through listening—to the silence, the music, the spoken word. Traditionally, the words used in anthems, hymns, Scripture, and responsive readings have been directed to the adult congregation. Many adults have difficulty with the language, to say nothing about the children. It is indeed a challenge to work out a service for worship that takes into account the needs and understanding of an intergenerational grouping.

When children are included in worship, attention needs to be given to the words they will hear. For example, if children are a part of the beginning of the service, the readings and music during that time will have simple, clear wording that relates to life today. Language that is abstract or symbolic will not communicate to the children. It is best to avoid using long readings of Scripture, long pastoral prayers, hymns with many verses, or complicated anthems. Not only is the child's understanding limited, but his or her attention span is as well. Some of the contemporary music has positive, happy messages. Children like these. Avoid melancholy, reflective music that turns into adult moods and requires a lot of life experience to appreciate. Modern translations of the Bible communicate better to children than archaic language does.

One way children respond in worship is through singing. A helpful plan is for the minister to select hymns that are appropriate both for children and for corporate worship. Perhaps a hymn a month could be chosen. During the month a particular hymn is being emphasized, it might be studied in the church school classes to enable children to sing it with meaning and familiarity in the worship celebration. In time children will recognize and be able to sing a number of hymns.

Very young children might listen to a recording or tape of the hymn tune while they play or do their creative activities. Although they may not be able to read or sing the words in corporate worship, they might recognize the hymn tune and respond with their feelings.

Children who are able to read usually like responsive readings. But they want to know which is their part! "Lining the Scripture" is an effective way of including children, especially those who do not read. The minister reads a selection of Scripture and pauses while the congregation repeats what he has read. Verses of praise from the Psalms or from the teachings of Jesus may be used in this way.

Through Sharing

There are several ways in which children may contribute to the worship service. Children may help to prepare the worship setting by decorating the sanctuary for special occasions. Examples include these: arranging wild flowers they have gathered on a hike; displaying banners they have made that relate to what they are studying and the theme of worship; cutting greens and arranging them for the Christmas celebration. Artwork that expresses the religious ideas and feelings of children could be duplicated for use on bulletin covers. The creative writings of children, such as poems, prayers, responsive readings, and new words to hymns, may be used in the worship service.

Children like to share in the rituals, such as the lighting of the Advent candles. In one congregation, the child chosen to light the candle is accompanied by a parent or another adult and a senior citizen who reads the appropriate Scripture. The intergenerational involvement helps to focus attention on the meaning of the act rather than on the child.

A group of older children was studying the meaning of the Communion service. They baked bread and brought it to the congregation as their gift for the celebration of the Lord's Supper. Because the children were present in the celebration, the minister substituted the following for the traditional words: "When you eat together, break the bread and remember Me . . .; when you drink together, remember what I have taught you. . . ." In that setting the children understood what Jesus meant and the importance of the celebration for Christians today.

In another congregation the older children dedicated a special offering for refugees. They asked the congregation to join them in moments of silence to pray for those who are homeless.

In one church school the weekly children's offerings are held till the end of three months. Then they are presented as a part of the morning worship in a special dedication ceremony involving all the members of the classes and the congregation.

Still another group of children taught a congregation a new hymn about the church. The minister gathered the children together and briefly mentioned their study of the church as community. Then the organist played the music. Next, the children, choir, and minister together sang the words that were printed in the bulletin. When it was the congregation's turn to sing, the children moved among the people, beckoning them to hold hands. As they sang, everyone responded by holding hands. It was not a formal act of worship, but at that moment the children, young people, and adults alike felt a part of one another—a true community. It was a "sharing" the children would not forget. Not only had they introduced a new hymn, but they had also experienced the church as community.

Through Leadership Roles

In one Canadian congregation the minister invites the children to help him lead in corporate worship. Every week he involves one of the older children. The child assists him in announcing the hymns and offering. The minister prepares the child by explaining exactly what she or he is to do and practices beforehand with that person. The same minister believes that younger children are able to be greeters and to pass out the bulletins. "Sure, it may take a little longer, but it makes the children feel important, responsible, included. . . ." Not all churches have a similar setting in which it is appropriate to involve children. Yet, on occasion, children may lead in the readings of the service and be helped to do it in such a way that enables others to worship.

Music is a natural way for children to participate in worship. It is not always possible to find enough children or the proper leadership to work with a separate children's choir. A small group of children, perhaps a class, might be involved in singing along with the adult choir. Perhaps they will sing only a part of an anthem or a refrain. Singing with the adult choir may take away the feeling of performing and, instead, may help the children to feel they are contributing to worship.

There are other ways children may be involved in worship. They may share instrumental music, present choral readings of Scripture, or dramatize Scripture through mime. Children are more apt to learn from experience than from example or observation in the worship service. They internalize what comes from their own involvement when they are enabled to feel, to understand, and to act out what they are learning about the Christian faith.

Chapter 2

Sharing with Children

The sharing times with children are those moments in the worship service when special attention is given to the boys and girls in the worshiping community. It expresses in an active way that children are essential in the Christian community's worship of God. On the following pages we will look at a number of ways to approach the time shared with children in worship.

A Word with the Children

"A word with the children" is a time when the pastor and the children talk with each other. Basically, it is a conversation time. The emphasis is on communicating with the young worshipers rather than directing ideas to lead to a particular teaching.

Usually the boys and girls move to the front of the church where they can be near enough to have eye-to-eye contact with the pastor. The pastor also moves to join the children and talks with them in a conversational tone that is warm and personable. Events that have been happening to children, their special interests become important during this sharing time. The pastor tries to tune in to their experiences and how they are feeling. Attention might be called to the arrival of a new baby, a visit from or to grandparents, accomplishments of children in music or scout activities, birthdays, projects, and so on. It could be an appropriate time to welcome a new child who has moved to the community. This might be done in a special way, just as we welcome new adults to the congregation in a special way. Long, involved sharing belongs elsewhere. "A word with children" is brief and uncomplicated. It lasts only a few minutes and may be ended with a prayer or the singing of a hymn. It serves to assure children that they have a place in the gathered community.

"A word with children" requires more preparation than it

would seem at first glance. The pastor needs to be flexible enough to set aside for a few minutes the content of the sermon outline that has been carefully prepared for the adult congregation. The pastor needs to be able to respond to what the children bring to this time.

But flexibility is not enough. Being able to relate to children in a personal way is essential. Yet, it just does not happen all of a sudden in that special moment set aside for communication. Here are some suggestions to enable "a word with children" to grow into a positive happening.

Know Who the Children Are

Relationships take time to build. As children are a part of the congregation of the church, they are also an important part of the church's ministry. Their needs are to be ministered to. The pastor will take the time, other than in the worship service, to become acquainted with them. It will take deliberate planning and hard work to do this. Building relationships with children cannot be done "off the cuff," as pastors are often able to do with adults. A good way to begin establishing relationships is to visit the church school classes regularly as a participant rather than as an observer. Sharing in the work and fun of camping and retreat experiences tends to build relationships, particularly with older children. Younger boys and girls will remember the pastor who came to visit them in their homes or who played games with them at the church picnic or other fellowship events. It helps to discover at what point the children are in their understanding and abilities. It is essential to know ways the community can help children's faith take shape and give it character. Their needs at different ages tend to be similar yet different. Certainly individual children have their own special needs. It is important for a pastor to be aware of the important changes that take place in the life of a child. Knowing each child in an individual and personal way helps the pastor to respond with understanding and with feeling to what the persons at this age bring to the worship service.

Be Prepared—Know What You Intend to Do

There is an element of risk in carrying on a conversation with children in a worship setting. One never knows what they will say! Spontaneous conversation may be natural for them, but it includes the danger of having unwanted information announced. We all know of times such as the time John was asked about his vacation. He replied in detail about how his mother was sick all night. Or when Betty told about the time her sister was so mean to her and her father screamed and yelled, saying some "bad words." Children often are realists. When they feel free and comfortable to talk in a church setting, they may bring up unpleasant incidents. Perhaps they enjoy the giggling responses they get from the other children or from the congregation. They may simply be innocent or honest enough to tell about that which concerns them.

It is best to have in mind the questions you will ask to direct the conversation. Rather than asking open-ended questions, such as "What happened to you this week?" ask "Do you recall someone showing kindness toward you this week?" or "We decorated the sanctuary yesterday for Christmas. Thank you for helping to make it so lovely. What do you like best about the decorations? What are you doing at home (or school) to get ready for Christmas?"

When one church was celebrating its anniversary, the pastor directed the conversation in this way:

Question: What do you see on the table in front?
Answer: A birthday cake.
Question: Whose birthday is it?
Answer: The birthday of our church.
Question: Can you guess how old our church is?
Answers: No. Ten years? Twenty years?
Pastor: Some of the members of our church were little children like you when the church was built.
Question: What do you like to do when you have a birthday?
Answers: Have a party! Eat cake and ice cream!
Pastor: Well, after the church service we will have a party. We will all have a piece of the cake to celebrate. . . .

The skills of being a pastor come into play in this special moment. Guide the conversation to avoid adding to the injured feelings of children whose lives have been hurt, for example, by the loss of a mother. The death of a grandparent or even a valued pet, for that matter, will be handled carefully and realistically. Children, like adults, have crises with which to deal, and the pastor will be sensitive to those feelings and needs.

Anticipate the Response

Trying to anticipate how children will respond is almost impossible. On the other hand, it is wise to think through how to handle some difficult situations.

Perhaps a new baby has arrived in one of the families. "Someone has good news to share," says the pastor. "Will you tell us about it, Jamie?" (No response.) The pastor continues, "A baby boy was born to Jamie's family this week!" "Oh, it's an awful thing!" interrupts Jamie. "It cries all night! I hate it." It happens to be an honest response from the boy. Of course, the congregation laughs at Jamie. The father and the grandparents sitting in the pews are embarrassed. How does one handle such a situation? Which is best: to make the child feel wrong about the feelings expressed— "Now, Jamie, you really don't mean that!"—or to identify with the child's feelings—"That is disturbing to you, isn't it? It does take time to get used to a new baby."

The following are some typical responses of children. What are the possible ways of dealing with each situation? A positive response is suggested for each situation. Keep in mind, however, that there is more than one good response. Each response needs to be fashioned to the individual child and situation. What if . . .

—A child tells a personal incident that should not be told.

> **Jane:** I'm tired! Mom and Dad quarreled so loud last night I couldn't sleep!
> **Pastor:** I'm sorry you are so tired, Jane.
> **Child** persists: Yeah, they yell and scream so none of us can ever get to sleep.
> **Pastor:** That does concern you, Jane. That is something we can talk about in private later.

—A child expresses hostility toward another child in the group

> **Jim:** Pete is stupid! I don't like him. I'm not going to sit by him.
> **Pastor:** You have strong feelings, I see. Perhaps you and I and Pete can get together and talk about those feelings when we are alone.

—The children will not talk.

> **Pastor:** All of us seem to feel quiet today. That is okay. It is good to feel quiet at times. Let us have a prayer together. (Or "There is one thing I would like you to think about today.")

—A younger child seems shy and begins to move behind the group.

> **Pastor** reaches out an arm to the child: Come, sit here with me. We want you up here with us. (If the child resists, the pastor may say, "Maybe you'll want to join us next week" and continue the story.)

—The children get turned on and will not stop talking. The talking gets out of hand.

Pastor: Oh, we all have so much to say. That's great! It is time for us to go back to our seats (or classes). We will talk another time.

—One child thinks she or he is a clown and needs to entertain the congregation while the other children talk with the minister.

Pastor: Joan, come here please so that you can listen better. We want you to come and to share with us.

When the unexpected happens, three important guidelines need to fashion the response:

1. *Focus on the feelings of the child* rather than on the unpleasant incident that has been reported.

2. *Affirm the child.* Avoid giving judgment or a moralistic lesson.

3. *Be positive and firm.* Communicate that you are taking the child (children) seriously but that the worship service is not the appropriate time to deal with a personal problem or to entertain the congregation.

It is easy to be embarrassed by what children say and to respond by laughing at them. But this seems to encourage even more "unsuitable sharing." Laughing *with* children is another thing. One might respond with "Oh, that was a wonderful surprise!" It is the sharing of happy feelings that counts.

Children can also be embarrassed when they feel adults are laughing at them. They usually become very self-conscious and often quit responding altogether. What does one say to a child when the congregation laughs at his or her comments? It is essential to communicate in different ways—by facial expressions, by touching, and verbally—that you are taking that child seriously. One might say, "Some of us have laughed, Jamie, but I know you are serious about that. It is important to you. Thank you for sharing it with us."

Although the special time with children has its uncertainties, it is a visible way to recognize and to affirm children within a congregation. It is a way for the children to be "active," other than by listening, in the worship service. Many think the purpose of "a word with children" is to provide an opportunity for the pastor to relate to children in a church family. As it has been suggested previously, the personal relationship between pastor and child needs to be developed on other occasions. During the special time with children, the pastor represents the church community in helping children to feel a part of the fellowship.

The "Teachable Moment"

The "teachable moment" is a time when the pastor leads the boys and girls in understanding a message of the Christian faith. He or she shares a learning to be remembered. It is presented in such a way that it relates to the life experience of the children and has meaning for them. Usually a story is told. (Chapter 4 considers in detail the use of the story with children.) The "teachable moment" may also be a conversation time, but one with a specific purpose, clearly intentional in its teaching. Sometimes a word, an idea, or a visual object is used.

Using a Word

A young woman pastor speaking to a school-age group of children used a word:

"Today I am thinking about a word that is important to you and to me. It is *recess*. How many of you have recess at school? . . . When do you have it?. . . What do you like best about recess?. . . Recess was an important time for me when I was in school. I used to get out into the playground and jump rope. It does make us feel good to exercise our bodies after we have been sitting for a long time in a classroom. Recess is like time-out from what you are doing. Sometimes it is having fun and recreation. But recess can also be time-out to be alone and to think about God and all the ways God shows us love. We may think of recess as a time to thank God in prayer."

Let us look at the word "recess" and the way it was used in the teachable moment. The word is certainly a part of the child's experience. It relates the gospel, the presence of the love of God, to an experience that is common to the school-age child. The minister focused on a single word and concentrated on a single event.

Using an Idea

A young father used an idea for the teachable moment:

"Yesterday I went to the ball game to watch my son's team play. It was a great game! We all got excited and shouted! You see, it was an even score for a long time. Then the other team got a home run. They won—right at the last part of the game!

Then something special happened after the game was over. All of the boys on both teams jumped up and down and shouted, 'Yeah!' 'Wow!' 'Great!' 'What a game!' 'Did you see Bill throw that ball?' The captains of both teams were patting each other on the back and shaking hands. *Well,* I thought, *this is interesting. Everyone seems happy, even the losing team.* I thought about it a little more and I think I know why everyone felt so good. You see, every member of both teams had a chance to play. Some players were not as good as others were, but that didn't matter. Each person had a chance to play and everyone had a good time."

To make a lesson out of this incident, shouldn't more be added? Couldn't we suggest, for example, that everyone needs to share in the life of the Christian community? This is not necessary; for in the single incident related to them, children may see the importance of giving everyone a chance to share in the game. It is the experience itself that is central to the child. When opportunities for children to participate and be involved along with others in home life and events in the church fellowship arise, the meaning of the experience in the incident may be recognized and transferred. The idea presented should be clear enough so that the "lesson" does not have to be pointed out.

Using an Object

A pastor used an object:

The pastor reached beneath the pulpit and brought out the well-worn treasure box while the children moved to the front of the sanctuary. It had aroused the curiosity of the children, from the smallest to the twelve-year-old, on many Sundays before. Opening the lid, he passed the box to each child.

"What do you see, Marie?" he asked the youngest in the group.

"A shell," Marie answered.

"Yes, this is a clam shell," he said. Picking up the shell, he proceeded to describe the life of a clam, how it obtained its food, and how the shell was its home. He related the object, the clam shell, to God's goodness and God's plan for life. The children were ready to recognize the teaching: "God cares for even the smallest bit of life, as God cares for you and me."

Numerous different familiar objects may be used. Puzzles, birthday gifts, pussy willows, or a picture of a church school class of long ago are all objects around which a lesson might unfold. Let the imagination run!

There is one important guideline to follow in using an object to teach. The meaning intended with its use must be clear and direct. Symbolic objects are not appropriate if the children must be mature to understand them or a longer period of time is required for teaching and learning about their meaning than is allowed in a worship service. Objects that relate to what the children know and experience are best. For example, young children know what an apple is. As they taste an apple and enjoy it, they may feel thankful to God. They may be ready to join in a prayer: "Thank you, God, for apples."

Be aware that just because children are interested in an object is not a sign that learning is taking place. Children are naturally curious. An object may attract their attention. However, one must always consider the following: *What lasting meaning does using this object have for the child?* The use of an object with children in worship is not to entertain but to convey meaning.

Using Words, Ideas, and Objects from the Bible

As we look again at the previous examples of the use of a word, an idea, and an object to teach, you will note that each begins with the child's experience and relates a Christian teaching to it. Many persons feel more comfortable using a Bible-centered approach. This, too, can be done effectively. The meaning of the material needs always to relate simply and directly to the child's experience today. The Bible and life should not be separated.

Here are some starters to help you think about using material directly related to the Bible:

Using a word: *love, praise, prayer.*

Using an idea: Jesus placed importance on children; Jesus chose fishermen, who were hard workers, to help him; Jesus was concerned for the sick and the poor.

Using an object: a scroll on which is written Scripture that Jesus might have read; a shepherd's staff; a picture of an event in Bible times.

The possibilities are endless.

Some Guidelines for the Time for Sharing with Children

The following suggestions will help to make the time for sharing with children worthwhile for boys and girls.

Be aware of how children understand.

It is quite possible that children may not understand about what the pastor is talking. The meaning may seem quite clear and simple to adults. But young persons have a different perspective. They may get an entirely different meaning that could be negative. Or they may tune out any meaning at all. We need to test whatever we say or use by asking these questions: How do the children see what is happening? What does it teach them?

The importance of how children learn, and especially of how they grow in the faith, has already been stressed. We have emphasized how knowing boys and girls as persons helps to direct our ministry to their growing and individual needs.

We need to avoid using abstract, theoretical ideas and symbolic meanings. Only a few of the preadolescents have developed intellectually to the point at which they can grasp quickly the deeper religious significance of words, ideas, and objects. Even older persons who are able to do symbolic and abstract thinking need more time to digest and reflect on meaning than is allowed for children in the few moments in worship.

Consider the age range of the children.

Each church will differ as to the number of boys and girls and the variety of ages included in the sharing time. We need to decide who will be included, because the readiness of children to learn is different at various stages. In many churches the younger children remain in the nursery during the worship service so that the group in the church includes the kindergarten and elementary-age boys and girls. In other settings the fifth and sixth grades are not included in the sharing time, particularly when there is a large number of smaller children in the church family. In smaller churches where there are few children, on the other hand, the sharing time may include a wide age span.

Use a method and subject that will reach all the children.

The wide range of ability to understand and the difference in interests and attention span do present a problem. These differences limit the meanings with which one can deal.

One teacher told how her fifth and sixth graders "had really gotten into social issues and problems." Their discussion came about as a result of a series of sessions in which they considered some of the teachings of Jesus. They looked at some contemporary problems and decided they could do something to minister to a need. They decided to contribute to funds to bring medical aid to a remote village in another part of the world. The children began to brainstorm: How could they earn some money? How could they involve the other people of the church in the project? At the height of their enthusiasm they had to leave to go into church service. About fifteen minutes later this energetic, "fired-up" group of boys and girls walked dutifully down the aisle to sit on the steps while the minister talked about "How nice it is that spring is here. . . . I saw a bird. . . . Oh, yes, and there are buds coming out on our tree. . . ."

The minister was presenting a *general idea* to reach all ages. If he had stopped to discuss the events of the previous hour with the fifth and sixth graders, the attention of the smallest children might have been lost completely. Yet the interest of the older children at that point was not with spring but with their project.

The previous example illustrates one difficulty in reaching a wide age span in a group of boys and girls. The following observed incident demonstrates another difficulty, the temptation to use "run-ons."

The pastor began talking to the youngest children about how Christmas is the celebration of Jesus' birthday. Then looking at the first and second graders, he realized they needed to know more than the birth of Jesus. He proceeded to mention Jesus' teachings and miracles to reach them. To give the older boys and girls a special bit of understanding, he touched on Jesus' death and resurrection. In this example we can appreciate the desire of the pastor to give meaning to each child present. Yet in trying to bridge the age gap, many ideas were presented. It is possible that no one direct meaning was caught by anyone. The discussion may have been more effective if the focus had been on the birth of Jesus who showed us God's love. The details of Jesus' teachings and the death and resurrection events need to be dealt with more carefully at another time and place.

It is easy to get carried away, to "run on" with ideas in an effort to teach each child something. It is better to use a general approach that focuses on one idea in a group of mixed ages.

Choose a subject that ties in with other themes.

The themes in the church school curriculum are sometimes unified across the age groups. Therefore, they will provide a source of ideas for the pastor to work with that are related to several ages.

In the illustration used previously, the teacher of the fifth and sixth graders might have alerted the pastor ahead of time to what the boys and girls were studying and their readiness to work out in their own way a ministry to the sick. The youngest children know what it is to be sick. They know how medicine and doctors help them to get well. They would understand the interest of the older children in wanting to help other boys and girls who would not have medical help. A story, simply told, about how Jesus ministered to the sick would have had meaning for the youngest children as well as the older boys and girls. It is helpful for the pastor to be in touch with what is going on in the various teaching/learning experiences in which the children are involved.

There are pastors who relate the children's moment directly to the sermon in the worship service. Families are then encouraged to talk about the similar ideas during the week. Many churches try to unify the theme of the church school and morning worship. This helps to reinforce and deepen the learning experiences. It also stresses the involvement of the total church community in a particular emphasis.

Check your preparation.

The task of providing for children in corporate worship often becomes a burden, especially when the other responsibilities of ministering to a congregation seem to be overwhelming. It is at such times that it is difficult to avoid some "common pitfalls." It is wise to check your preparation by asking the following questions.

How is your approach positive? A positive approach is affirming to children. It leads them to an understanding of the gospel that frees them to grow. Boys and girls respond when they are left not with a sense of guilt, but with a good idea that they can use in their living. Moralizing is not necessary. All teaching needs to be clear; however, a leader does not need to stress why he or she is using a particular idea.

Who will hear the message? One often notes adults commenting, "The best time of the service is the children's time. I like those stories." However, getting a message across to the adults through the children is not a purpose of the children's moment. The teaching is intended for the young persons.

How does the material you have prepared for the children's time minister to them? One pastor wrote an imaginative, creative series of stories in which the main characters were birds with human names and human follies. It was highly symbolic and unrealistic. The adults loved it! As the pastor began the "children's story" from behind the pulpit, the congregation usually chuckled in anticipation. The boys and girls sitting in the pews not only missed the words that were literally spoken over their heads, but they also missed any appropriate meaning. Without being aware of what he was doing, this pastor was promoting his creative ability and was being encouraged by the congregation. He needed to ask himself: *What am I doing through these stories that ministers to the young worshipers? How am I ministering to them on behalf of this church community?*

Evaluate.

Keep a careful record of what is used in the children's moment each Sunday. Record in detail what was used and note the children's response to it as well as how much time it took. At the end of several weeks look back over what you have done. What pattern or theme emerges? How was the Bible used? How were the stories child centered? Which moments were most effective and for what reasons?

Variations for Sharing with Children

There are a variety of models for sharing with children in corporate worship. One pattern involves the children in an act of worship.

In one small congregation in which the children remain for the entire worship service, the pastor asks them to come forward in the middle of the service. After greeting each one by name, he joins in a circle with the children. As they hold hands together, he prays with them for their common concerns and then prays for each one of them separately.

Another pattern has been observed. The children come into the worship service during the closing moments. Coming from their classes, they bring something specific to share with the minister and the people in the congregation. They talk about what they learned or activities they participated in within their teaching/learning situation.

One church, with carpeted floor and flexible seating, has designated an area in a corner of the sanctuary as "The Children's Place." There is a low, round table, around which kindergarten and younger elementary children and an adult sit, on the floor, during the latter half of the service. A variety of quiet activities is offered to the children. This church wants its children to feel a part of the church family at worship and to experience something of its beauty, ritual, music, Bible reading, and the caring of people.

"Learning in Worship" is the program of a church that believes that "*in* worship is the primary place that learning *about* worship occurs." Each week the chuch staff prepares a study sheet with four activities for children to do during worship. The study sheet, a pencil or crayon, and anything else that may be needed are put in a kit that is handed to elementary school children as they enter the sanctuary. All of the activities relate in some way to the sermon and/or the theme of the service.

A separate family worship service has proven more suitable in some situations. All ages from babies to senior citizens participate. It is usually informal and planned around family concerns. Boys and girls often share in leading the service. Family worship is usually brief and held prior to the church school or before the more formal service.

In all of these examples, we see boys and girls being affirmed in the household of God. Adults are also being made aware of the value of children and their own responsibility in enabling them to grow in the Christian community. There are different ways to share with children in worship. The pastor and congregation need to plan for the most appropriate model to meet the needs of the children in the worshiping community.

Chapter 3

The Importance of the Setting

The setting is more than physical environment. It is what is created by those who gather. It is the combination of people, their leader/pastor, their attitudes toward and expectations of the worship experience. It does not matter whether the worshiping community meets in a schoolroom, in a room in a home, in a dark, antiquated sanctuary, in a huge cathedral, or in a bright, cheery, modern structure. It is the experience of God's presence that counts! It is the joyous reverence that people together feel toward God that is important. The setting has an effect on the child's response in worship and particularly in the children's moment.

Corporate worship has been described as the celebration of the active presence of God and involves the response of persons and the community to God. How is this experience enabled in a worship service?

Stiff formality, rigidity in pattern, and stuffiness inhibit the person's ability to become aware of God and one's own desire to respond to God. These characteristics may encourage a personal response that is automatic, a behavior that is expected. This is not to say that the traditional pattern of worship is not viable. How the pattern of worship frees the person to experience the presence of God is what matters. This is true also in those settings where an effort is made to establish a feeling of community through informality and "chattiness" between the congregation and pastor. In many circumstances, corporate worship has become the chief time for building a feeling of community in the church. Creating a "town meeting" atmosphere focuses on people. The purpose of worship is to celebrate God.

Freeing Persons to Worship

Each congregation has its own unique style of worship. In our concern to create an effective worship experience that involves children, we want to ask: Is there a "freed up" atmosphere that enables them to share in worship? The following questions need to be examined by a worship committee as it plans for the diversity of worshipers that gathers on any given Sunday.

• What is the pattern of the worship service?
• What are the purposes of those who lead the service?
• What is the attitude of the people toward worship?
• What do the members of the congregation understand about the meaning of worship?
• How does the congregation respond? Are they like visitors, observing the event in a proper manner, or participants, helping the event to happen?

What the pastor and congregation expect to happen is critical. Their understanding of their respective roles in enabling worship is important. The children catch what the community feels and understands. What children sense is happening will direct their own awareness of and response to God in worship.

The following traditional Protestant worship service was observed by visitors. What might the boys and girls have experienced in it?

The service began only when the minister arrived. As he entered the sanctuary the organist began playing as a sign for the people to rise in respect. He took his place on a platform above the congregation; this platform was as high as the balcony. From his high position he directed the people in the usual hymns, responsive readings, and prayers in the order of worship. There were no other persons involved in leading worship, neither lay persons nor a choir. In this setting it was easier to be an observer than a participant in the event. It was as if the minister were a play director giving cues for the actors to say the right words at the proper time.

Children sitting with families also seemed to be observers, passively watching the movements of the leader. There was no squirming or fussing; the children exhibited proper behavior from all that one could see. The children's hymn was announced. As one might expect at this point, it was adult centered in wording and concepts. No recognition was given to the children's actual presence, nor was there an opportunity for the boys and girls to share in the experience in a way that had meaning for them. It appeared to be a negative experience for the children. When the time came for their exit, they did so hurriedly, as if to escape to a happier place.

This may seem to be an extreme example. However, it is a worship pattern that occurs repeatedly in churches. There are dangerous characteristics in this illustration that may be found in other worship services. What is happening to children in such a situation? Physically, they are uncomfortable. They need to strain their necks to see the minister who is situated up high. Because he or she is leading the worship alone from the high pulpit, they see the minister as a powerful figure. He or she is the authority. He or she controls what happens and tells people what to do. These small children feel insignificant in the pews. None of the words spoken or sung is in the everyday language they know. It is difficult for them to sense worship as celebration. Their awareness of a loving God is clouded by the powerful figure of the pastor. There is no opportunity for them to respond in worship on a level that crosses their lives.

How could we turn around what is happening to the children and adults in this particular illustration? What are some positive ways persons might be helped to become involved in corporate worship?

First of all, the physical position of the pastor and congregation in this setting is crucial. The only alternative in this sanctuary is for the pastor to come down from the high pulpit to face the congregation on the main floor. This would help him to establish eye contact with persons in the congregation, particularly the children. He might then seem more human, real, and less in "control" of the worship experience. Sharing the leadership with others, lay persons and/or a choir, might help those in the congregation to feel it is the community at worship; it is their act of worship together, rather than the minister in control of worship. Children as well as adults need the models of lay people participating in the leadership of worship to sense it is a community experience. Most important is the inclusion of children in some way in the worshiping community. Children need to tune into something they understand, whether it is a hymn, a prayer, or a special time when they are recognized by the pastor. They need to be enabled to respond in worship on their own level of understanding.

The setting for worship needs to be such that persons are comfortable and free to respond in their own ways. Congregations often expect the pastor to be solely responsible for enabling worship. The people must also share in creating a worshipful atmosphere.

Adults may have to take a second look at the boys and girls in their midst to realize the rights of children within the worshiping community and to make room for the language and experiences that have meaning for children.

The Readiness of Adults

Much has been said about the readiness of children to experience worship. Let us also think about how ready are the adults to enable children to worship. Both the pastor and the adult congregation need to understand the purpose of the presence of children in corporate worship.

An honest discussion of the place of the child in worship may lead to understanding. A committee made up of the pastor and lay persons who represent Christian education and programs of worship and growth might discuss whether or not and how children should be included in corporate worship. Things to discuss include:

• When and how have children been included in worship?
• In what ways have the children themselves been involved?
• What are the values of a special time with children in your situation? What makes it meaningful for the boys and girls? For adult members?
• What is the attitude of the adults in the congregation toward sharing with children?
• How is the children's time a distraction in the worship experience? How could it become an integral part of the worship experience?

Adults become more sensitive to the needs of children when they are involved in making decisions as to the place of the child in worship, when the children's time will occur in the service, and who will lead it. It is far better to have persons ready to support a time for children in the service than to proceed without such understanding.

Introducing the Children's Time in Worship
The Timing

The children's moment may become a part of each Sunday service or happen occasionally. When it is a new addition to the worship service, it may be best to include children only at special times. Special occasions such as family emphasis days, Christmas, Easter, and the celebration of a church anniversary are appropriate times. Particularly when there has been a traditional worship service that excluded children, the children's moment may be more readily accepted by the congregation when it is introduced slowly.

In some congregations there may be a number of persons who do not understand the presence of children in the worship service. Yet, at the same time, there are several younger families who do appreciate the open sharing of children and their need to be a part of corporate worship. The feelings of each will be respected.

A Shared Ministry

"Why does the minister have to be good at everything?" asked one laywoman. How true! We expect the minister to be flexible and able to lead well in every area of the church's ministry. It is assumed that the pastor will lead the "Sharing with Children" time. However, in many congregations there are lay persons who are able to tell a story or carry on a dialogue with children.

One pastor reports, "In a recent worship evaluation survey done in our church, we asked for volunteers to assist the pastor in the worship segment we call 'Through the Eyes of a Child'. Several persons did sign up and I will be working with them during the year. A team approach surpasses an individual effort because it includes more creative minds and enriches the effort through a mix of experiences and approaches."

Lay people, carefully chosen because of their understanding of children, may communicate valuable insights to boys and girls. Their sincerity and readiness to share something important of the Christian faith will be caught. Their participation represents the community, the "people of God," ministering to its own, the children!

Church school teachers, educators, parents, older children, young people adept with guitars or puppets, senior citizens with stories of the church's history in mind all have something to share. Guidelines for selecting material and instruction on how to use stories of the church's history in mind, all have something to share. could be provided for participants in the children's time. The time limit is also an important factor to stress. Lay people assisting with the children will find it helpful to know the focus of the pastor's sermon and the theme of worship in order to tie in their contribution.

What has lay participation to do with adult readiness to enable children to worship? When lay persons are involved, they bring their personal witness to children. When they share in this meaningful task, they become more receptive and ready to support the ministry with children.

A Parent's Dilemma

An option for parents to leave very young children in nursery care during corporate worship should be given. These are the words of one mother who needed this option. "Each child is different. Now, with Alan, I would not have minded if he stayed with me in worship. He could sit still and be good. But it would have been so much different with Amy. She never sits still for a split second. She would have been in the racks of the pew, into the hymnbooks, climbing on the seats. There would not have been one moment of peace for me or anybody else sitting near me. I would rather not go to church if Amy had to be with me." There are parents who are not comfortable with their young children present. Some children are so active, they need to have separate care. The time for very young children to be in the worship service usually needs to be limited.

Parents also need to be prepared as to the purpose of the presence of their children in worship. Amy's mother may have been so conscious of her exuberant behavior that she communicated anxiety to Amy. Parents need help in understanding that children need to be accepted for what they are in the worship experience and not be made to imitate proper adult behavior. This is not to say that children will be allowed to misbehave or deliberately to annoy other persons. Young children especially need activity and attention. When both are denied, they rebel.

Developing Adult Readiness

To help adults understand boys and girls and accept their presence in corporate worship, we must keep them visible as a part of the total life of the Christian community. Some ways to do this have been mentioned in regard to involving children in contributing to corporate worship. There are other ways to keep adults aware of the children:

1. Include children in as many activities in the life of the congregation as is appropriate.

2. Display on bulletin boards children's artwork, pictures of children participating in learning activities, recreation, camping. A bulletin board that has displays that frequently change will attract attention.

3. Share some of the writings of children (with their permission); their poems, prayers, and songs may help others to understand how children learn and express their faith.

4. The pastor and lay leaders may call attention to the

importance of the ministry with children through sermons and discussions.

When adults are convinced that it is important to share corporate worship with children, they will sense a new dimension in their own worship experience. They may see their own contributions to the lives of children. They may come to know the freshness of understanding that children bring in their ministry to adults. Children may help adults to celebrate God's gift of life and life together in community.

What Children Bring to the Setting
The Feelings the Children Bring

The feelings the children bring to the children's moment determine the meaning it will have for them. Young children respond first through their feelings. When their needs for security are satisfied and they are comfortable within a pattern, that is, they know what to do and what is expected of them, they are more ready to respond. They also feel what others communicate by their actions. Uncertainty about themselves and suspicion of their surroundings develop when adults give children scowls and shake their heads with, "I wouldn't do that. . . . No! No!" They need affirmation and acceptance of who they are in order to be open to the worship experience. As children grow, they become aware of adult attitudes toward worship. They know well what importance the congregation puts on their participation and respond accordingly.

On Display

Young Peggy was reluctant to join the children in front of the sanctuary. "I don't want people to make fun of me!" she told her mother. Peggy was just five years old, but she was already conscious of the people in the pews who laughed at the boys and girls. She did not like that, as we might understand.

Children often feel they are on display for the adults. They often make the most of the situation by waving to grandparents, smiling broadly to friends in the congregation, or showing how clever they are by teasing others or saying something to rouse a response from the pastor or congregation. This kind of reaction is difficult to get hold of and turn around so that children become only aware of the leading of the pastor at that moment. Some suggestions for dealing with such situations follow.

The Pastor with the Children

The arrangement of the children for this special time can make a difference in their responses. The pastor will want to move to be near the boys and girls to avoid speaking to them from behind the pulpit. The children also need to be in a position where they are facing the pastor rather than the congregation. Being able to see each other eye-to-eye will help communication. When boys and girls are seated in the front pews behind one another, they may feel as though they are in school. They may feel they are being taught or talked down to. They may also find it more difficult to share their ideas in this more formal setting. When this is the only possibility for seating, it places more responsibility on the pastor to communicate warmth and to effect rapport with the children.

More often we find the children sitting on the steps facing the people and the pastor sits with them. This arrangement is really not best for either pastor or children. It is difficult to look directly at each of the children and to keep their attention away from themselves and the people they see in the congregation. It is natural for the boys and girls to feel self-conscious in this position. They either retreat and become shy, or they will show off and say things they normally wouldn't say. It would be better for the children to sit on the floor with their backs to the congregation, while the pastor sits on the steps facing them. In some large churches the children gather off to the side of the front of the sanctuary with their sides to the congregation. The pastor then looks away from the congregation and faces the boys and girls. A suitable arrangement is not too difficult to find. Children usually accommodate easily to any situation, especially when their basic needs are kept in mind. The children will need to feel comfortable, to be at ease with the pastor, and to be able to pay attention.

Using a Microphone

How boys and girls respond when a microphone is used is another consideration. The need for and use of a mike must be evaluated carefully. A lapel mike may be needed to enable the children to hear. If this is necessary, other factors may need to be examined. Perhaps the size of the group needs to be limited by excluding the very young or the older elementary children. Or perhaps it is a matter of how the children are gathered that affects the ability to hear. One needs also to question the use of a mike for the congregation's benefit. (While the children's time is for the children, the adults should be able to hear even though the pastor's motive should not be to give a simple lesson to the adults through the children's story.) The problem with using a hand mike is that it makes the pastor seem like a master of ceremonies. Speaking through a mike is like speaking through another person and not directly to the children. However, a tiny lapel mike can be unobtrusive and overcome the acoustical problems of a large sanctuary. Used carefully, a mike may not make children feel on display, nor will it obstruct the desired personal sharing relationship.

The Pastor Enables

The pastor's relationship with the children is crucial in sharing with children. As one pastor explained, "I try to treat the children as equals. I try not to patronize them or to talk down to them. Above all, I don't tell them to sit down in the front pew and to be quiet. This would be the worst thing I could do." This same pastor has an unusual rapport with the boys and girls. He knows them all by name and is concerned with how they feel about themselves and their role in the church. The children know what his intentions are in sharing with them. This pastor can be trusted to create a situation in which the children do not feel self-conscious.

Another pastor feels that the children are important in the church family, but does not like the idea of calling the children apart in the worship service. "I feel as if I am treating them like 'second-class' citizens. Of course, I am not able to produce a sermon with ideas to include their thinking. But I still hesitate to speak to them separately." This pastor first needs to deal with his own understanding of children in worship. The children will sense his attitude and feelings of being uncomfortable with them. All that is expected from him from the child's point of view is a sincere concern for their sense of belonging in the community. They do not need a "watered down" sermon, but just a word of assurance that they are loved and a part of the people of God.

The Older Children

Older children tend to be self-conscious, especially when there are more smaller children present in the children's moment. Fifth and sixth graders may need to be treated more like adults than the younger children. Opportunities for them to share through drama, choirs, instrumental music, and so on, may be more appropriate for their involvement. (See page 18.) In order to have a special time for children in smaller congregations, however, it is usually necessary to include a wide age span from nursery-age children to the twelve-year-olds. One way to involve older children in such situations is to enlist them as "caretakers" of the very young children. As "caretakers" they gently guide the children to the front of the sanctuary. They sit with them and, if it seems natural, they may even hold some of the small children. Afterwards they walk with the young children back to the pews or to the Nursery Class. Preparation for this role is done ahead of time. The pastor needs to help the older children to understand how the "caretaker" role contributes to the sense of community within the church fellowship. This might be done either in the church school class or in personal conversation. When older children seem reluctant to participate in the children's time, it is a clue that they need to be recognized and involved in corporate worship in other ways.

Building Feelings of Belonging

Children are more open to what is happening when they feel they belong to the church family. Younger children recognize the smiles, the hugs, and the understanding looks when pennies roll across the floor during a prayer as ways of saying "You are special!" The senior citizens in one church made an effort to sit with any child who was attending a service without family, friends, or teachers. In this way they acted out their acceptance of children in worship. Friendships developed between young and old as a result of their caring. The children also felt more a part of the community at worship.

A "celebration" committee in one church felt that building a sense of community within the church family needed to be emphasized. To meet this need committee members planned around the theme of celebrating the people of God. The theme was developed through several weeks and involved the children in their church school and in corporate worship.

On one Sunday morning the elementary-age children were busy finding out who the people were who came to worship. They had cut out circles for name tags. As the young people and adults came to the sanctuary, the children invited them to sign their names on one of the tags. They took the initiative to introduce themselves and explain what they were doing. It was done in a way that was quiet, orderly, and not distracting from the atmosphere of worship. Later the children gathered the tags and placed them on a huge banner that was made to symbolize the community in their church. It was placed on a wall in the sanctuary for all to see. Another activity included taking pictures of individuals and family groups during a social hour. The older children attached the pictures to branches that made up a tree. During this emphasis the sermon in the morning worship centered on the idea of community—the people of God in the Old and New Testaments and the importance of the Christian community today. The children's moment was tied into the overall theme.

The total emphasis helped the boys and girls to get acquainted with some of the people in the congregation and to come to know their own importance as a part of the church family. This learning experience enabled them to worship with the community and to be ready for their special time in the worship service.

Helping Children to Understand the Feelings of Adults

Children are able to become sensitive to the feelings adults bring to worship. They may experience how the people of God share the feelings of joy, sorrow, tension, and anticipation of one another and bring these feelings into the act of worship. Children may become aware of God's love shown through the caring community.

The study of prayer and the place of worship in the Christian community is important. As children grow in their ability to comprehend meaning, we will help them to realize the purpose of corporate worship and how the order of service is planned to guide people in the worship experience. When they contribute to corporate worship, we will help them to understand how they are enabling a worship experience rather than performing for an audience.

One young man of twelve read the Scripture in a beautiful, effective way. Many adults were astounded with his reading ability and the feeling he put into the Scripture. When asked "Have you had voice training? Where did you learn to read so well?" he replied, "You know Mrs. Anderson always sits in the back row. She is blind. My dad helped me to realize how important it is for her to hear. I wanted her to be sure to hear the message of the Scripture." As children learn to respect the feelings of adults in the worship service, they, too, will contribute to the setting. They may come to the children's moment expecting to get something out of it.

Chapter 4

The Story and the Storyteller

The Use of the Story

Children have been listening to stories for many generations. Long before words were written down, human history, cultural values, and religious beliefs were passed on through stories. Children, as well as adults, sat at the feet of the storyteller of the clan or tribe to hear about adventure, heroes, past events, customs, and practices that were important. Most likely, Jesus as a boy in Nazareth learned much about the Law and prophets through the storytelling of the elders. Jesus himself used parables, a form of story, to convey meaning. Today, as in the past, storytelling is an effective method.

The Use of the Story with Children in Corporate Worship

Stories may be used to do many things: to entertain, give information, prepare a group for a project. In Christian education the story is used as a means of guiding children in Christian growth. When told to children in worship, the story is used to communicate one particular meaning to the children. Although the story may have the effect of enabling a worship experience, its chief purpose is to convey one thought or one idea that is usable in the children's experience.

What Makes a Story Good to Tell?

How does one go about choosing a story? What are the characteristics of a story that will appeal to children and get across the point?

Stories used as part of a worship experience for children are more effective when they are *realistic*. That is to say, there needs to be that element in a story used in a worship setting that allows for the child to think or feel, "That is familiar. . . . " "Aha, that happened to me. . . ." "I feel that way too sometimes!" "I could do that!" The meaning we intend to communicate through a story is one that has direct relationship to the child's experience.

We will avoid any kind of approach that may cause children to associate religious meanings with fantasy. If they come to associate religion with fantasy, they may hang on to this identification for the rest of their lives. We do not want to confuse the child's mind in this way. Fairy tales, for example, are often complicated, symbolic, and have a deeper meaning than is seen on the surface. Surely they do have their place in the life of the child and may be appropriate in other settings. Imagination is the stuff out of which good stories are made. However, stories with strange, unfamiliar settings and grotesque or strange characters do not have their place in the worship setting with children.

Stories need to be realistic, possible in actual life.

Relating the Story to Children's Experience

When choosing a story for children, try to see it through the eyes of children and not from an adult perspective. The best story paints a picture of life that the children can quickly see in their mind's eye. It needs to be written well enough so that as the story unfolds, the children will be able to imagine its characters and happenings.

For example, children in North America will not readily understand a story that involves the customs of an African tribe. And it may be difficult for children in the city to respond to a story that relates circumstances common only to a rural setting. Likewise, out-of-date stories that involve experiences that would have been common to children even ten years ago are lost without a detailed explanation. Stories introducing life in another time or place do have their purpose. They broaden the experience and awareness of children. However, in the limited time available children may miss the intended focus. Stories that require a lot of explanation of an unfamiliar background are more suitable in another type of learning experience.

Since the sharing time with children in worship does not provide the time or atmosphere for dealing with the customs and background of the Bible, special care is needed in selecting Bible stories for use in worship. We will choose Bible stories that can have meaning for children without an understanding of the time and place from which they came.

The element of feeling that the story provides is also important. Children need to be able to identify with the feelings of the characters as they move through the events of the story. They should be thinking as they hear the story, "I know what it is to feel that way." Stories built around a common experience that is realistic will interest children.

The best story paints a picture of life that a child can quickly see in her or his mind's eye.

Making Stories Appropriate for All Children

Stories need to be appropriate for the age and interests of the children gathered. Children differ in their ability to understand. Stories need to be told to fit the abilities of different ages. In our enthusiasm to share the Good News with children, we often give too much too soon! We need frequently to remind ourselves that children are at different developmental levels and their understanding differs accordingly. Jean Piaget provides us with help at this point. Piaget's conclusions are based on at least fifty years of careful observation of children. According to Piaget there are three stages in the child's intellectual growth: intuitive thinking (*approximately* 2-7 years), concrete thinking (*approximately* 7-11 years), and abstract thinking (*approximately* 11 years on). Let's examine how these stages apply to the children we know and the material we will use with children.

The stage of intuitive thinking includes children ages two to seven. Children of this age do not have the ability to think logically. They think in separate little bits that are not connected. For example, watch a small child opening a gift. The child seems more fascinated with the ribbon, the paper, and the box than with what is inside. The connection between untying the ribbon, taking off the paper, opening the box, and discovering the gift is not made. The mental association is not made unless the child has had lots of experience opening gifts. Another example is seen in a nursery child who, as he went to church with his parents in England, was told "This is God's house." When he moved to Canada and was taken to another church, he asked the question "Does God have lots of houses?" He probably was surprised to think that God had moved to Canada, too. It was beyond his ability to understand God as an ever-present being who might be worshiped in many buildings around the world. At this stage the child is unable to link one thought with another. The young child is able to celebrate the birth of Jesus for it relates to the child's own experience of knowing babies and having birthdays. Talking about Jesus as a boy who lived in a family also makes sense to the intuitive-thinking child. Younger children are aware of how "big" they are growing and their own experience in a home. However, they will not be able to follow the events of Jesus' life from birth to resurrection. Nor will they understand the religious concepts underlying biblical material.

The stage of concrete thinking includes children ages seven to eleven. Children in this group are beginning to think logically, and for the first time they can also trace the steps of their thinking. For example, they may plant seeds and connect the importance of soil, water, and sun to the growing process. In contrast, younger children will follow the same steps, as directed, in planting a seed, but they will not be able to identify the importance of proper care. Usually we have to prevent young children from drowning the seeds with water.

The elementary children who think in concrete ways recognize the events that happen but not the underlying, symbolic meaning of those events. Take the Christmas story as an example. As children read and hear about the presence of the shepherds, the kings, and the angels, they know that the birth of Jesus was an extraordinary event, a special happening. They may follow the events in Jesus' life, such as his questioning the elders in the temple when he was a boy, his decision to be baptized, his reading in the synagogue to announce the intentions of his ministry, and so on. However, they will not understand the significance of Jesus as the promised Messiah. Children in this stage are not yet able to distinguish the event from the meaning of the event itself. Another example may be seen in how the children understand the gathering of Jesus with his disciples for the Last Supper. They may understand the importance of the event, the fellowship of Jesus and his followers, but they will not grasp the symbolic meaning of the bread and wine offered during the meal.

The stage of abstract thinking includes children ages eleven years and up. Most often children at this age are able to think logically and are growing in their ability to handle abstract, symbolic terms. They are better able to grasp the hidden meanings of, for example, Jesus' parables. They may see in the Christmas story the significance of Jesus' coming as the Prince of Peace. They are growing in their sense of history. So we will want to guide them in their understanding of Old Testament material, Jesus' life and ministry, and Jesus Christ as the fulfillment of the messianic hope. These older children are able to understand the biblical material on a more conceptual level than the younger children do.

We recognize that not all children fall into these categories at the appropriate ages. Individual differences do exist. The influence of the home, school, the part of the world a child is growing up in make a difference in that child's ability to handle concepts. However, considering these stages of growth will help us to choose material for stories to use with the children.

Stories for a Group with Many Ages

How does one choose appropriate stories to meet the various levels of understanding for children in a mixed group? First, the material used will have a teaching that may be caught by children at different levels of understanding. The story of Zacchaeus has such possibilities. This story has much to teach. However, the open, loving friendship of Jesus toward a person who was lonely and despised can be communicated to children of all ages. The theological and moral implications of the story, such as the justice of tax collecting and the forgiveness of sins, are far beyond the young child's ability to grasp. Emphasis can be placed instead on the feelings of Zacchaeus, the people, and the genuine love of Jesus.

Developing themes that cross the life experience of all age groups is a good approach. For example, caring (the sheep and the shepherd in Psalm 23), friendship (Jonathan and David), and Jesus' attitudes toward persons can be shown through stories. Some examples show Jesus' attitudes toward women, children, the sick, and the poor.

Different age groups will sometimes identify with different aspects of a story. Stories centered around the things Jesus did, such as the visit to the temple when he was twelve or blessing the children, can be understood by different age levels. Let's use the visit to the temple as an example. The youngest children will be aware of their own experience of going to church with the family. They will understand that the boy Jesus also liked to go with his family to worship. Middle elementary children may be interested in Jesus' daring to ask questions of the elders. They, too, are of an inquisitive age. They often ask important questions about the church and can identify with the interest of Jesus. The older children may sense in this event the special meaning that Jesus' life had a unique purpose.

If one gears the Bible story to meet the interests of the oldest children, it is obvious that the younger children will be lost. On the other hand, telling a story that is quickly understood by the youngest in the group may have the potential of meaning for the older children.

Conveying Meaning Through the Story

A story told to convey meaning will have a *lasting quality* about it. The truth will be remembered long after the story is forgotten. The learning or insight may be adapted or transferred to other situations as the children grow in their life experiences. The story will not teach anything that has to be unlearned, anything that is inaccurate or untrue. Stories that are not based on an actual incident will be clearly identified with a qualifying phrase such as, "Once upon a time. . . ." "This story never really happened, but it is one I want to tell you. This is a story that *might* have happened."

The story will have *one single theme* that is easy to recognize. The temptation when creating a story is to pack as many lessons into it as possible. Avoid such a temptation. Those who regularly write sermons around three points will need to realize that a story for the children needs only *one point* underlying the unfolding events.

Putting the Story Together

A good story will be *put together well*. The beginning quickly introduces the persons in the story and the background. Where it takes place and the problem involved are set forth in such a way as immediately to grab the curiosity of the listeners.

The action part of the story, sometimes referred to as the body, tells about the happenings in sequence. Here the character(s) are involved in events that move in orderly fashion, smoothly from one to the other without interruptions. Children like stories that move fast. Subplots, flashbacks, or passages that distract from the problem or the main theme will lose the interest of the children. Boys and girls also respond to stories that have a certain amount of conflict. "What will he or she do?" Suspense holds the interest of the hearer. (Younger children require little suspense.)

The climax of the story brings to a head the crisis—the decision to be made, the solving of the problem. This is the turning point in the story when the listeners know exactly how everything is going to turn out. Then the story comes quickly to an end.

We often tend to be compulsive about adding our own ending by pointing out the lesson in stories to children. A good story will involve the child's imagination, thinking, and feeling to the degree that the meaning becomes obvious to the child. A good story will be strong enough to make clear the message to the child without the teller needing to tack a moral or lesson to it.

Painting Vivid Word Pictures

The *language* will paint vivid pictures in the minds of the children. Words will have pleasing sounds. Young children, especially, like a sense of rhythm. They also like words that awaken their senses of taste and smell. The story will be told in such a fashion that it lends itself to conversation among the characters as it is told. Using direct discourse makes a story come alive, makes it seem as though it is happening right now. We might say that a good story will turn on the "memory recording" in the minds of both the teller and the hearer so that *who, when, what, how,* etc., are clearly pictured.

Making Stories Move Quickly

Plan for stories that move quickly from beginning to end. The children's moment in corporate worship is brief. A rough rule of thumb for a time limit is to allow one minute per age of the youngest child in the group. (For example, if the youngest child is usually four, plan to limit the story length to four minutes.) Stories that need more explanation or discussion should be told at another time.

Like the Story Yourself

Whether the storyteller really likes a story or not is rather important in story selection. When you like a story, it is much easier to breathe life into the characters and let them present a "live" incident and a learning to be remembered. Children are very perceptive and will "hear" what the storyteller "says" with facial expressions and tone of voice, as well as what is spoken.

Selecting Bible Stories with Care

The Bible must seem like an awesome book to children. Even to those children who read, it may appear to be a strange, different kind of book. For it is a book they cannot pick up and read from cover to cover easily and readily understand. The Bible is a book written by adults using adult language. So much of the material is unsuitable for children because it deals with adult happenings. Many of the personal experiences are far beyond the child's understanding and daily experience. Yet, even young children are able to know that the Bible tells us about God's love. They may not know the words being read from the Bible in corporate worship, but they can sense how important it is for adults. To help children have an open, positive attitude toward the Bible, stories told or created from biblical material need to be chosen with care. Children will grow to value the Bible when the stories they hear deal with life as they experience it today.

While other stories will have been written especially for children, the Bible was written by and for adults. Therefore, it is necessary to select and/or adapt Bible stories for use with children. The biblical material used should be chosen to have a direct meaning to the child's life. The most appropriate Bible stories for children have something that children can pick up and put to use in their own daily living. To help you choose appropriate Bible material for stories, refer to the chart, "The Meaning of Bible Material from the View of Children of Different Ages," on pages 54-63.

Any Bible story that is told to children in corporate worship should have the characteristics of a good story, discussed on pages 45-52. Perhaps to test the value of a Bible story you want to tell, you might ask "What is the meaning of this story?" "What will the children learn from listening to the story?" "What ideas of God or Jesus will they gain?" "What lasting meaning or quality does the story have that will grow with the child?"

Choose Bible Material for Its Intended Meaning

In using the Bible with children, we try to present the meaning as it was intended both in Bible times and for our day. As children grow, we want them to discover deeper meanings and not to have to "unlearn" shaded interpretations of biblical material.

To help convey both the biblical meaning and the current meaning, consider the following suggestions.

• Recognize that the storytellers in Bible times told stories to get across a meaning or express a feeling, not necessarily to pass on a record of historical happenings. Most of the stories were intended for adult understanding; they were told to convey profound underlying meanings. If these stories are told to children as true happenings, often the emphasis falls on the details of the story rather than on the meanings they may have for the person. Noah and the ark is a good example of a story often misused and overtold. It is easy to tell, especially with all the detailed descriptions of the boat, the animals, etc. With children the details of the story can stand in the way of the truth behind the story. Certainly the element of God's judgment and mercy, the importance of the covenant of Noah with God are intended for adult understanding. However, children do know what it is to make a mistake and to have another chance. They can tune into the experience of Noah that God does understand, forgive, love, and give us a new beginning.

• Identify a Bible story by introducing it with a statement such as: "This is a story we find in the Bible."

• Avoid taking a verse out of context to create a story.

• Try to be as accurate as possible regarding biblical customs and historical background when creating a story.

• Stories created about Bible times should always be identified with "This is a story that might have happened in Bible times."

• Be cautious in using contemporary words, or slang, that seem clever, but that may alter the original meaning.

• Be aware of how you use words that may have a negative meaning for children or may create prejudices toward people today.

The Meaning of Bible Material from the View of Children of Different Ages

Old Testament	Young Children (Intuitive—what is real at the moment)	Early Elementary (Logical thinking)	Older Elementary (Beginning to think abstractly)	Categories, Themes for Stories, Conversations in Worship Moments
Abraham Genesis 12:1-9	New experiences; the uncertainty and confusion of moving.	May understand Abraham as a person who trusted God, who moved out.	God's covenant with Abraham; understand what faith means from Abraham's responding to God's call.	God's love people of God myself feelings choices
Jacob Genesis 25:27-34; Genesis 27:25-29; Genesis 32:22-31	In a family there may be two different kinds of persons, such as the brothers Esau and Jacob.	Differences between the two boys; Jacob's cheating Esau; Jacob's experiences that changed his life and made him a person through whom God worked.	Humanness of Jacob: fear, loneliness, sense of failure of the fugitive; God's purpose was fulfilled in a man who had done wrong.	people of God God's love myself feelings choices friends
Joseph Genesis 37:3-11; Genesis 41:39-46	Coat of Joseph represents the favor of the father; oldest brothers jealous.	A character study of Joseph:—proud and arrogant. An unusual person who developed faith, patience, generosity; trickery of brothers; feelings	God is able to work through Joseph; God helps Joseph (people) grow and change.	people of God God's love myself feelings choices

David and Jonathan 1 Samuel 18:1-4	Know what a friend is.	of jealousy; forgiveness. An example of friendship.	Meaning of friendship: what goes into a relationship.	myself feelings friends
Amos Amos 7:7-8; 10-15; 2:6-8; 4:1-2; 5:6; 6:1-8	A person who loved God and was concerned about other people.	A herdsman who loved God and believed God wanted him to speak out against the injustices of the time; events in preaching; meaning of a prophet—a spokesman for God, a brave man who risked his life for the sake of others to speak out for God; ways we help today.	Can understand the moral values involved, social justice; realize God's desire for social justice today; ways people of God are responsible today.	people of God caring and sharing feelings choices
Jeremiah Jeremiah 1:4-7		May understand that the people were not acting as they should, as God expected them to behave (worship of other	God's call to a young man; what Jeremiah preached; young persons today can help others to know God.	people of God feelings choices caring

The Meaning of Bible Material from the View of Children of Different Ages

Old Testament	Young Children (Intuitive—what is real at the moment)	Early Elementary (Logical thinking)	Older Elementary (Beginning to think abstractly)	Categories, Themes for Stories, Conversations in Worship Moments
Jeremiah (Continued)		gods); may identify with Jeremiah's feelings (Jeremiah 1:6). Know a prophet is a spokesman for God.		
Poetry and Hymns of the Psalms that relate to the experience of children: Psalm 1:1-3; Psalm 119:9-16; Psalm 34:11-14		The Bible helps us to know how to live a good life.	Experience of those in Old Testament times is that following God's way brings happiness.	people of God myself feelings caring thanksgiving
Psalms 8; 100; 104	The young child knows awe and wonder of the natural world.	Feelings of gratitude to God the Creator; God created persons "special" to care for the world.	Greatness of God as seen in creation; dignity of man; persons are responsible for creation.	
Psalm 23	May be aware of the care of sheep and the task of a shep-	May identify with the feelings of the shepherd toward the sheep	Understanding of the shepherd's faith in God growing out of	

herd.		in his care and his trust in God to guide him.	personal experience; may recognize God's care in his or her life.	
Psalm 84	May like going to church.	May understand the feelings expressed about going to the temple; may relate to similar feelings we experience in the Christian community today.	Understand the importance of the temple worship; may sense the joy of the worshiping community.	
New Testament **Birth of Jesus** Luke 2:8-14; Matthew 2:1-12	May know the anticipation of a birth in a family setting and the joy (or uncertainty) of the arrival of a new baby; know birthday celebrations; may identify with the joy of the arrival of the baby Jesus and the celebration of his birthday.	Celebrating birthdays are important; can follow the sequence of a person's growing up from babyhood to adulthood; are able to understand Christmas as the celebration of Jesus' life: one who possibly helped his carpenter father; probably went to the synagogue school; went to the temple; showed us God's love.	Realization that Jesus was God's Son; celebration of the totality of Jesus' life and mission.	Christmas myself sharing love with others

The Meaning of Bible Material from the View of Children of Different Ages

New Testament	Young Children (Intuitive—what is real at the moment)	Early Elementary (Logical thinking)	Older Elementary (Beginning to think abstractly)	Categories, Themes for Stories, Conversations in Worship Moments
Jesus' Visit to the Temple Luke 2:40-52	Understand the meaning of growing to be big enough to go to church; may have had the experience of learning about God in church; can understand how Jesus grew to be big enough to go to the temple with his parents.	Children have many questions about God, Jesus, church, prayer, etc.; are able to understand how Jesus would be curious and ask questions of the elders in the temple.	May recognize the unusual inquisitiveness of Jesus; may understand Jesus' awareness of his mission.	events in Jesus' life myself church
Friends of Jesus Fishermen Mark 1:16-20	Know what a friend is; know that there are different kinds of people in the world and different kinds of work; able to understand that Jesus chose fishermen as his friends to help him with his	Becoming aware of the meaning of friendship: need to share, trust, etc.; can understand the work of fishermen (physical, hard work; danger; willingness to risk); may understand how Jesus needed	Jesus needed followers who were willing to take risks; Jesus did not simply choose the "acceptable types" or religious leaders to be his friends and helpers; commitment costs.	friends/helpers of Jesus commitment choices caring and sharing

Story				church myself feelings
Simon Meets Jesus Luke 5:1-11	May know the work of a fisherman.	friends, helpers, and people who had the qualities of the fishermen to help him.	Children may have the opportunities to share in the work of important tasks at school, home, or church: they know what it is to be counted on to be a good worker; can see how Jesus needed to choose strong, dependable people like Simon to help him; miracle is not stressed as much as Simon's trust in Jesus and recognition of the importance of Jesus' invitation to follow him; may be able to think about the nature of Simon's promise (commitment) to work with Jesus.	
Businessman Mark 2:13-17	Know what friends and helpers are; aware of different kinds of work.		May be aware of what taxes are, how people may have negative feelings about paying taxes, and their feelings toward tax collectors; can follow the events in the story and may understand how the "teachers of the Law" did not approve of Jesus' associating with the businessmen, but would rather he associate only with those representing religion.	
Jesus and the Children Matthew 18:1-5; Mark 9:33-37; Luke 9:46-48	Children need to be loved and to be affirmed; may understand that Jesus loved the children and was their friend.	Have a need to be loved and to be considered important; from their own peer group experiences can relate	Jesus' ministry was for all people; children are important to the Christian community.	

The Meaning of Bible Material from the View of Children of Different Ages

New Testament	Young Children (Intuitive—what is real at the moment)	Early Elementary (Logical thinking)	Older Elementary (Beginning to think abstractly)	Categories, Themes for Stories, Conversations in Worship Moments
Jesus and the Children (Continued)		to the argument of who is the best in the event (Matthew 18:1); can see the value Jesus gave children.		events in Jesus' life feelings choices
Death of Jesus Matthew 27:27-50; Mark 15:16-39; Luke 23:25-46; John 19:17-30	May have experienced separation from parents, grandparents.	May have experienced death in family or among friends; understand there were those who were against Jesus and wanted to kill him; can understand the feelings of disappointment and confusion among the disciples and followers; determination of Jesus to do what God wanted him to do; his refusal to deny that he was God's Son (emphasis on event).	Jesus knew God's love so completely that he was willing to endure death to allow God's love to be real to humankind.	

Easter Matthew 28:1-10; Mark 16:1-8; Luke 24:1-9; John 20:1-18	Know feelings of joy at the return of a friend, reunion with parents; experience the wonder of new life emerging in the natural world.	Understand that what Jesus taught about God's love and how God wants us to live in love will never die.	Beginning to appreciate the hope of life after death.	celebrating life God's love as seen through Jesus Christ
People Jesus Helped Simon's Mother-In-Law Mark 1:29-31	Children know what it is to be sick in bed; they know how worried their parents or caretakers get when they are ill.	May identify with how Simon felt because his mother-in-law was ill and how happy everyone was when Jesus made her well; recognize in the events of the story Jesus' helpful attitude toward others in need.	Recognize Jesus' unique ability to heal; awareness that they may help others; able to make plans and carry through with them.	Jesus' attitude toward others myself caring and sharing choices friends
A Leper Mark 1:40-45	Children are aware of persons who are helpful, e.g., doctors, firemen, ministers; may see Jesus as a person who helped others in need.	Miraculous emphasis is avoided; may plan and carry out ways they can respond to the needs of others.		

The Meaning of Bible Material from the View of Children of Different Ages

New Testament	Young Children (Intuitive—what is real at the moment)	Early Elementary (Logical thinking)	Older Elementary (Beginning to think abstractly)	Categories, Themes for Stories, Conversations in Worship Moments
People Jesus Helped (Continued) Jesus and Zacchaeus Luke 19:1-10	May experience meeting people for the first time; may know what it is to feel shy, strange, lonely, or afraid of meeting others; may understand Jesus as a friendly person.	Aware of others who are not accepted or may themselves experience rejection by others; may see how Jesus expressed forgiveness and acceptance of Zacchaeus; may explore ways they can show acceptance of others.	May understand that love made it possible for Zacchaeus to feel good about himself and to make amends; may understand that Jesus represents the redeeming love of God.	
Stories Jesus Told The Lost Sheep Luke 15:3-7	May understand the care of a shepherd for sheep; may experience caring for own pet; may know what it is to lose something valuable and the joy of finding it.	May understand what was involved in "shepherding" for the Palestinian shepherd; may relate to the feelings and concern of the shepherd; may understand the meaning of each one being important to God.	May understand the love of God for each person; recognize that God is forgiving; may raise the question "Who am I in relation to God?"	the teachings of Jesus myself caring and sharing

The Lost Coin Luke 15:8-10	May know what it is to lose something and how happy one feels when it is found.	May relate teaching to God's love for each person.	God's love is for all people; God wants us to show our concern and care for others, whatever the differences may be.	feelings friends choices caring and sharing
The Good Samaritan Luke 10:25-37	Know what it is to be helped when they are hurting; may be able to consider others who are in trouble (who have fallen off their bikes, lost a note to take home from school, etc.)	Aware of differences among people as to their willingness to help others; may relate the meaning of the story to how they may help others.	May understand apathy: seeing, but doing nothing.	
A Boy Who Helped Jesus John 6:1-14	Know the feeling of being hungry for a meal; understand people were hungry and that a child shares his lunch.	May see the problem in the situation, i.e., many people with no food or money; may recognize the importance of the boy sharing; miracle is not stressed as much as the spirit of giving/caring.	Children can share in the Christian community and the ministry of the church; application of the importance of sharing and caring in our ministry today.	friends of Jesus feelings choices caring and sharing church

Creating Stories from Everyday Happenings

The world around us provides a bounty of sources out of which children's stories may be created. The storymaker needs to be aware of the experiences children have and must be able to see these happenings through the eyes of children.

From Where Do the Ideas Come?

1. *Listen to the children.* Children have a wealth of information to share. As adults, we often miss what they are really saying. We tend not to take them seriously. Yet, in the everyday experiences of

Creating Stories from Everyday Happenings

Listen to the children. . . .

children, we may find evidences of the Christian message. Listening is a skill. Listening to children requires concentration and patience. When relating on a one-to-one basis, the child needs to know that he or she has your sole attention. Your schedule or agenda has been put aside. It is the child's time to talk freely. As a listener, one will avoid finishing sentences for the child or interrupting with "I had that happen to me once. Let me tell you. . . ." or "Now, when *I* was your age. . . ." A listener asks questions or rephrases what has been said to encourage children to talk. Tuning into the feelings underneath what is being said is also important. A five-year-old boy may seem to talk excitedly about the first day of school. The feelings underneath may be those of apprehension and insecurity.

Listening to children can give us ideas for stories. Their conversations will be held in confidence. However, they might serve as thought provokers to creating stories that deal with life as children know it.

2. *Observe events.* What do you see happening around you in families, in community events, and in church occasions that affects the lives of children? What are the meanings of these events that could be woven into a story?

Let's look at family life. First, there are the special occasions: a new birth, birthdays, reunions, accomplishments and honors that come to family members. Then there are the problem areas: loss of jobs and financial insecurity, family breakups, death. We know that the time limit in the children's moment is *too* limited to deal adequately with the crises children are facing. On the other hand,

Observe events. . . .

stories may be created about situations that have meaning that can be significant to what the child is experiencing. For example, all children are in need of physical and emotional security, particularly as their world keeps changing. A story about a person who discovers the supporting love and care of people in the fellowship of the church or in the community can be reassuring. A story focusing on how a child coped with a difficult situation may have something to say to a group of children who experience prejudice because of their racial/ethnic backgrounds.

Stories about persons or events that were significant in the building of a community or a church may be useful. They will need to have elements of suspense and action to hold the attention of the children. Older persons often can be the source of tales of events that are exciting and adaptable to a children's story.

3. *Recall your own personal experiences.* What you know best is what you have experienced. Granted, a series on "When I was little . . ." can be boring. There may have been significant happenings in your life, however, that can become the basis of a good story.

Recall your own personal experiences. . . .

4. *Remember exciting people in Christian history.* Here again, let us remember that children like stories that are on the move and do not have a lot of detail. Children will not learn history in the children's moment, but may catch the spirit of commitment and courage that our forerunners had. Stories about historical figures will emphasize their decision making, problems they dealt with, and their daring to do what they felt God meant for their lives.

Remember exciting people in history. . . .

Be on the lookout for news. . . .

5. *Be on the lookout for news.* Letters from missionaries or news items in the current papers are good sources for story ideas. A missionary's dangerous journey to save the life of a child can be told in an exciting way to children. Newspaper captions, such as "Boy Finds Pet for Elderly Woman," "Determination Wins for Judy," "Children to Hold Fair," are starting points for creating a story.

The storymaker will choose an idea carefully for the purpose and meaning it will communicate to children as it is woven into story form. The story itself will be created from a child's viewpoint.

Tips for Writing Your Own Story

First:

1. Decide on an idea or an incident that can be developed into a story for children.

2. Determine the one point the story will stress.

3. Think through how it will begin and how it will end.

4. Outline the action, step by step.

5. Pinpoint the conflict.

6. Think how suspense might be created.

Then:

1. Write a beginning that gets into the story immediately.

2. Write a description of the action. Do this several times, and then check the one that best gives the feel of movement in the story. (Which is better: "He ran as fast as he could to . . ." or "He thought he had better run quickly . . ."?)

3. Write out the conflict. Do it so that the words create tension.

4. Write out sentences that tell the suspense.

5. Go back over what you have written and write conversation into it as much as is possible.

6. Write out the climax; how was the problem solved? This should be simple, brief, and direct.

7. Write a conclusion. It needs only to be a sentence or two.

A Word of Caution

Be sensitive to the effect of the story on children.

1. *Do affirm children* with stories that help them to see how it is possible to cope or to make a similar decision. Do tell stories with situations that are not too close to what the child is experiencing in problem areas. A child should be led to think, *Yes, I could do that, too,* not *He is talking about me (or my family).* Nor should a story embarrass children because it is an actual incident that happened to them.

2. *Do give a positive direction* to the children. Do not overload the child's sympathies. For example: When telling a story of how a group is providing help for a child suffering from hunger, it is enough to emphasize how help is being made possible. The details of the causes of hunger—being orphaned, being a victim of war, etc.—are conditions for which the children are not responsible. Nor should they be made to feel ashamed or guilty because they are not suffering, too. Avoid saying, "Michael doesn't have a place to sleep or good food to eat like you have. . . ." It is better to show how help for the hungry child is made possible and how the children may also contribute.

3. *Do help the child's need for security.* Don't set up fears by telling stories about incidents that children do not understand or that present worrisome ideas. For example, don't tell about a child who was taken away from parents because they could not care for her properly.

4. *Do let the story tell the lesson.* A story with appropriate meaning for children will not have a moral tacked on to it. Nor will it lay an unrealistic burden on the children. For example, one pastor ended a story with "Now, you go and do the same. . . ." One child replied, "I wonder if I can; that is just too much!"

Techniques for Storytelling

Successful storytellers are able to get inside the story and make it come alive as if it were actually happening at that moment. They like what they are doing and like the story they are telling. One does not have to have a particular personality to be able to tell a good story. The teller, however, does need the ability to forget oneself and become immersed in the story that is being told.

If for any reason the story does not seem easy to tell or does not appeal to the teller, it is better to find another story. The storyteller will show by his or her enthusiasm that there is value in the story being told and beckon the attention of the listeners.

Preparing to Tell the Story

1. *Be clear about the purpose for using the story*. The story being used in the children's moment needs to teach one single idea. Read the story carefully to check whether or not it really does meet your aim. If it is a Bible story, read it in its biblical setting to understand the background and its context. Ask, "What prior understanding will the children need to have to gain meaning out of the story?" (If too much is required, is it, then, a good choice?)

2. *Decide how the story will begin*. The first few sentences are important. They need to capture the interest of the children immediately. If necessary, improve on the beginning of the story. Rewrite it from different starting points to find the most interesting beginning. One way is to get into the story from the perspective of one of its characters.

For example, consider the story of the healing of the sick man who was let down through the roof of the house where Jesus was (Mark 2:1-12). Look at the people who are involved in the story. How could you begin from their point of view? The story might be told through the experience of:

a disciple;
the man who owned the house;
an onlooker, someone listening to Jesus;
the man who was paralyzed.

As another example, use the incident of the boy with the loaves and fish to share. A story might be told through:

the boy,
a disciple,
one of the crowd.

Once the beginning is decided, then the events of the story will follow and lead to a quick climax and conclusion.

3. *Make an outline of the story*. Note that stories have four main parts: the introduction, the action, the climax, and the conclusion.

Jot down under each part phrases or words that are picturesque, whose very sounds help to make vivid the feelings and action. Rather than "He was mad," use "He grumbled!" Rather than "He could see in her eyes that she was happy," use "Her eyes sparkled with joy!"

4. *Picture the scenes of the story* in your mind's eye as they appear in your outline. People are visually oriented. If you can see

the story in scenes, you will be better able to paint those scenes with words in the child's mind.

5. *Tell the story to yourself several times.* Use your imagination to tell the story in your own words. There may be parts you wish to memorize. Be cautious, however. Memorizing a story could make it mechanical, unreal. Imagine the characters as real, live people living out a happening. Use as much direct conversation as possible. Hearing the characters talk helps the story come to life for the children.

6. *Practice your speaking skills in storytelling.* Your voice is important. Easy, deep breathing is good to develop. Deep breathing helps the voice to be full and flexible in its ability to change pitch or adjust the pace. Speak in a natural tone, but project the voice so that all can hear. The beginning words spoken with an intimate tone will catch the attention of each child. To avoid being monotonous, use a variety of ranges wisely. Changing the speed and emphasizing particular words may create interest. The effective use of one's voice can:

—show how a person feels through descriptive words or phrases, direct discourse;

—imitate sounds;

—give a feeling of movement;

—point out a conflict;

—build a climax.

Use of pauses also helps expression. Pauses may be used to:

—build suspense;

—heighten tension;

—indicate a change of time in the story;

—point out the conversation in the story before or after a character speaks;

—introduce a new character;

—emphasize descriptive phrases.

Careful use of gestures and body language can be helpful in telling a story. Gestures should be natural and spontaneous, used only when they are related to the story. The storyteller is not an actor performing before an audience. Overdramatic gestures with hands or the body will distract from the story. Facial expressions— smiles, downcast looks—can communicate how the characters feel. The position of the body can also communicate the moods of the characters: stooped shoulders and head down (feeling sad); back straight, shoulders up, head high (feeling good.)

Avoid the Pitfalls in Storytelling

Telling the Story

Each storyteller will develop his or her own special style. It will come through deliberate practice. Some helps for success are:

1. *Be comfortable.* You and the listeners need to feel physically comfortable and natural in the setting. All the children need to sit where the storyteller can be seen and heard by everyone.

2. *Create a listening mood.* The storyteller needs to have a manner that is both dignified and friendly, that says, "I have something special to tell you." Developing a ritual in the children's moment, when the children know it is their special time, will help. This may be a hymn or the pastor's announcement. Prefacing the story with a chattiness to effect a rapport with the children does not always work. They may respond by being talkative and get out of the mood to listen. Waiting and pausing till everyone is in place and ready to listen is a good way to begin. Look at each child to gather attention before beginning.

3. *Get right into the story.* Your beginning words are important. Recall the emotions of the story. Begin with words and a tone of voice that quickly introduces the story.

4. *Speak clearly and distinctly.* Use a pace that is suitable for the story and gives the children a chance to keep up with you and the action in the story.

5. *Move quickly* through the beginning, the sequence of events, the conflict, the solution to any problems, and the end without interruptions.

6. *Focus attention on the story and the message it carries.* The story is presenting the idea; therefore, story helps such as pictures and objects are usually inappropriate for the "sharing time" in corporate worship. Children may be distracted with the presence of story aids and miss the impact of a well-told story. When objects are used, they tell the story.

Storytelling in the children's moment can be most effective. As stories bring to life the experiences of others in the past and present, children may learn how to respond and to cope with their own life situations. When the children are ready to listen and the pastor (or other persons) are well prepared to tell a good story, there are the possibilities for growth and worship.

Our Ministry with Children

In the preceding chapters an effort has been made to consider our ministry with children in corporate worship. It is hoped that some things have become clear.

First, it is essential that we plan with care for the various ways in which children may become involved as persons in the worshiping community. This means we will take seriously their need to be participants in an intergenerational group. We will consider how they understand the faith so that they may take part to a degree that will have meaning for where they are in their own life experience.

Secondly, as we explore the ways to help children experience worship, we realize the necessity to examine our own attitudes toward children in corporate worship. We are urged to look at the worship setting that either inhibits or frees persons who gather to worship, the flexibility of the worship service that may involve children in some way, and how the pastor and other persons may relate to the children.

Thirdly, practical ways to create a meaningful sharing with children have been suggested. The constructive use of conversation with children, as well as using a word, an idea, or an object to facilitate a "teachable moment," have been suggested. The story as a method has been described in detail to help the pastor or person leading the sharing time to develop skills in the art of storytelling.

Of course, no one way or method is best. Whatever works most effectively in a particular congregation needs to be used. It is possible that using a variety of ways will create a worthwhile sharing time. On the following pages resources are provided. Some of these may be used as printed; others will provide ideas that may be developed.

As we celebrate God's gift of life and life together in corporate worship, "let the children come" with their openness and childlike faith. Then our awareness and response to God in worship together will be enriched.

What follows is a collection of stories, gathered from many different sources, for use with children in corporate worship. The stories are arranged in eleven categories, but their use is not necessarily limited to one area.

Pastors and others who have the responsibility of planning for a time for children in corporate worship are urged to collect their own stories and ideas to add to what is here. It is the hope of the planners of this book that this resource section will help and inspire you in your ministry with children.

Resource Section

Special Days and Seasons

New Year's Sunday

Gift of Days

On the first Sunday of the new year I brought the past year's calendar with me. "I have with me this morning a calendar, and I'm wondering if one of you would take the calendar and tell me what date it is today." Several of the older children took the calendar and, after some study, figured out it was the wrong year.

"What's wrong with this calendar?" I asked. "It's the wrong year, isn't it? Just a few days ago this was a useful calendar, but not today.

"Was last year a good year for you? What made it a good year?

"Well, if 19 ___ (last year) was a good year for you and for me, why don't we just repeat the year and postpone 19 ___ (the new year) for a while? Why can't we do that?"

We discussed that time only goes forward. It can't be postponed or stopped. "There's only one _____ (today's month, day, and year). It only happens once. This day, ____ (today's date), is a gift. Who gave it to us?" (The children responded that God was the giver of days.)

"Let us thank God for this gift.

"God, we thank you for the gift of each new day. Help us each day to be more like you want us to be. Amen."

Stephen Jones

76

Epiphany

Three Kings Day

January 6 is a special day in the church year. It is called *Epiphany*. Did you know that long, long ago there was no Christmas to celebrate the birth of Jesus? Instead, Christians celebrated Jesus' birth and baptism on January 6, and the day was called Epiphany.

Three or four hundred years after Jesus lived, Christians began to celebrate the birth of Jesus on December 25. We all know what that day is called! Christmas!

Epiphany, which comes at the end of the twelve days of Christmas, continued to be an important day for Christians, even though the birth of Jesus was now celebrated on a different day. Epiphany celebrated one event that is usually celebrated as part of Christmas. Does anyone know what it is? (The visit of the wise men.) Even though the story of the wise men is often told as if it happened on the day Jesus was born, we know now that Jesus was about two years old when the wise men visited him and his family.

Epiphany is a reminder of that visit. It is a sign that Jesus is the Savior of all people. It is a time to think about our responsibility to share the good news of God's love with people who have never heard of Jesus.

Almost every country has developed stories and customs for Epiphany. One of the legends says that when the wise men went home they gave up their important jobs, distributed their possessions to the poor, and preached about Jesus. That is what Epiphany is all about!

(It would be appropriate to follow this story with the singing of a hymn about the wise men, such as "As with Gladness Men of Old" or "We Three Kings of Orient Are.")

Elizabeth W. Gale

Martin Luther King, Jr.'s Birthday

Walk Together, Children

"Daddy, why do white people treat colored people so mean?"

asked Martin Luther King, Jr.'s son when he was six years old.

His father must have wondered, *Will my child ever be treated as a person rather than judged by the color of his skin?* Martin Luther King, Jr., remembered when he, too, was a small boy and had asked the same question. One day he had gone shopping with his father to buy shoes. Together they sat down in the first empty seats at the front of the store.

"I'll be happy to wait on you if you move to the seats in the rear," said the clerk.

Martin's father refused, saying, "Either we buy shoes sitting here or not at all!" The shoe clerk refused to sell shoes to the dignified black Baptist minister and his young son. Angrily walking out of the store, his father vowed never to accept a system that did not treat blacks equal to whites.

It may have been that and other childhood experiences that led Martin to spend his life in trying to change the unfair treatment of black people. Martin Luther King, Jr., became the leader of the freedom movement.

Members of the movement began not to ride the buses because blacks were not free to sit in the white section of the buses, even if there were empty seats. After 382 days the city officials passed laws to allow blacks to sit anywhere in the buses.

This success brought hope that other rights could be won for black people, and Martin Luther King, Jr., started the Southern Christian Leadership Conference to work for the rights of all people. King continued leading "sit-ins" and marches. The people were abused because they took a stand against the discrimination shown to them. King trained the people to resist without fighting physically. They accepted the name-calling and did not strike back. They were kicked and cursed. The police used dogs and fire hoses on the peaceful demonstrators. Men, women, and even children were put into jail. In one instance a black church was bombed, and four children attending church school were killed.

King was jailed many times. His life was threatened. Phone calls came to his house with threats of killing his family. In spite of the danger, Martin Luther King, Jr., would not give up because "he had a dream." He told about his dream in a speech to a crowd of 250,000 blacks and whites in Washington, D.C. Over and over again he said, "I have a dream. . . . I have a dream that my four little children will one day live in a nation where they will not be judged by the color of their skin, but by the content of their character. I have a dream that one day little black boys and girls will be able to join hands with little white boys and girls and walk together as sisters and brothers."

Martin Luther King, Jr., gave his life to try to make his dream come true; when he was only thirty-nine years old, he was killed.

His dream of blacks and whites walking together must not be forgotten. Will you help to keep it alive?

Adapted by E. W. Gale from Arline Ban, *Baptist Trailblazers* (Valley Forge: Judson Press, 1980), pp. 39-41. Used by permission.

Valentine's Day

Valentines Mean Love

(Prepare in advance a large valentine with four small folded red hearts pasted on it. Each heart is folded to cover a word—*love, others, God, ourselves.*)

(Show the large valentine.) When you see a valentine, of what do you think? (Love. Reveal the word "love" under the center red heart.)

What does it mean when you say you love someone? (You do things for them, give gifts, etc.) Whom do you love? (Summarize answers as "others" and reveal that heart.)

As Christians, we have also expressed our love for whom? (God or Jesus. Reveal that heart.)

There is someone else who needs to be loved. Who do you suppose that is? Ourselves! (Reveal this heart.)

Valentine's Day is named for a man named Valentine who lived a long, long time ago—about three-hundred years after Jesus. Valentine loved God and wanted to live in a way that would please God.

One day he seemed to hear God speaking to him, saying, "Help the people nearest to you." One thing Valentine did was to make people of all ages happy with gifts of flowers from his garden. He moved among the people of his village performing acts of kindness, especially to those who were sick or sad. He was known and loved by everyone. People said he was like Jesus because he helped them know God.

Some people say that after he died his friends wanted to remember him in a special way. So on his birthday (February 14) they sent notes or gifts to people in honor of their friend Valentine.

Today, seventeen hundred years later, the example of Valentine reminds us to love God, other people, and ourselves, as Jesus taught us to do.

Adapted from material contributed by Richard Sammer.

First Sunday in Lent

Lenten Bread

This past Wednesday we began a special time in the church year. It is called *Lent*. Does anyone know what happens during Lent? (Fasting, praying, and giving up something all occur.)

There is a story about Lent that I would like to tell you.

Many, many years ago—in fact, way back in the fifth century—people weren't allowed to eat milk, eggs, and fat during Lent. That meant forty days plus Sundays without bread. That meant no pancakes, no cake, no donuts, no pie, and no cookies.

One day a baker in a town in Germany got to wondering about something that could take the place of bread. He decided he would try to make something.

He tried a lot of things. After several tries he finally put together just the right amounts of flour, salt, and water. He had a kind of dough. And then he thought to himself, *I can't make this into just an ordinary shape. This should be a special shape to remind us what Lent is all about. . . that it's a time to prepare for Easter, that it's a time to pray.* Then it clicked; the idea came. He took the dough and rolled it out, twisting it several ways until finally he had it just the way he wanted it. It was twisted in such a way as to look like two arms crossed in the act of prayer.

And he gave it a name. What do you suppose he called it? (A pretzel.)

For many years after that, pretzels were given to people on Ash Wednesday in Austria, Germany, and Poland. And they were eaten only during Lent. They were eaten to remind people of the real meaning of Lent.

We eat pretzels throughout the year and some pretzels have changed their shape. But when you see a pretzel like this, it can remind you of what Lent is all about.

Optional ending: I have brought some pretzels with me today so that we can each eat one and think about what Lent means. But first, let's share the pretzels, because Lent is also a special time to share. (Children pass pretzels to the congregation and then eat their pretzels.)

Linda Isham

Palm Sunday

Joshua's Flowers

Joshua and his mother lived in a tiny house outside the city of Jerusalem. Since he had been a tiny boy, Joshua had loved flowers. In his little garden he had many different kinds of plants which he had brought down from the hillsides. Each morning as he watered them and loosened the dirt around their roots, he talked to them and called them by name.

On this particular bright spring morning, the flowers seemed lovelier than ever. But Joshua was troubled. He was thinking of Eli, the storekeeper in the city who had passed by a few days before.

"Those flowers are very nice, Joshua," Eli had said. "I could sell them to the visitors who come into the city. Bring some of those white ones to the marketplace in a few days, and I will pay you a fair price for them."

Before Joshua could reply, Eli had moved on down the road. Now as Joshua watered his flowers, he was remembering Eli's word.

"I don't want to sell you," he said to the white lilies, "but Eli has promised to pay me well. And just think of the wonderful things I could buy for myself if I had some money." Joshua's heart was heavy as he cut the lovely white blossoms. He wrapped the stems in large, wet leaves. Holding the lilies carefully, he started down the road toward the city.

He hadn't been walking long before many people began to gather along the side of the road. Some were carrying large, leafy branches; others were singing and shouting.

"He is coming, he is coming," they sang as they waited.

Joshua was puzzled about this.

"Who is coming?" he asked a little boy who was running along the road.

"Jesus is coming. See, there he comes now!" replied the little boy.

Joshua looked down the road to where the boy was pointing. A large crowd of people were walking beside a man who was riding on a little donkey. They waved their branches and sang, "Hosanna, Hosanna! Blessed be he who comes in the name of the Lord!"

But Joshua scarcely noticed the people. His eyes were on the face of the man who was seated on the donkey. It was such a kind face, but the dark eyes had a troubled look in them.

"He is sad about something," thought Joshua. "And he looks so kind. How I wish that I might do something to make him happy."

Just then Joshua remembered the lilies in his arms. In a second he had left his place at the roadside and was running close to the people who walked by Jesus. Taking care lest the lilies get crushed, Joshua pushed through the crowd until he was right next to the little gray donkey on which Jesus rode.

"Here," he whispered, as he ran along beside him. "I want you to have these." And he thrust the lilies into Jesus' arms.

"How lovely," the man whispered back. "Thank you, Little Friend."

Joshua stepped back quickly to the side of the road. He stood and watched until the crowd disappeared through the city gates. Then he turned and began to skip along the road home. He no longer had his lilies, and there were no silver coins jingling in his pocket, but Joshua didn't care.

"He called me 'Little Friend,' " he sang happily, over and over again. "He called me 'Little Friend.' "

—Based on Matthew 21:1-11

Adapted from Mary Smucker Hulburt, "Joshua's Flowers," *Children's Religion,* April, 1952.

Easter

Easter Morning

Mary Magdalene and Mary, the mother of Jesus, and Salome couldn't wait. For them the night had passed too slowly. Before daybreak they got up. Through the streets of Jerusalem they walked while it was beginning to get light. For one last time they wanted very much to be with Jesus. He had been their best friend while he was alive. Now that he was dead, they wanted to honor him once more.

As they hurried along, they remembered how Jesus had helped them to happiness.

Those red lilies of the field, thought Salome. *I always knew they would be there every year just as surely as the spring would come. I didn't think much about them at all. Then one day Jesus was telling how God takes care of us. He said that even King Solomon with all his splendid clothes wasn't dressed as well as one of those lilies. After that I saw them with new eyes. They looked beautiful. And life has changed for me like that—from something common to something glorious.*

Mary remembered how her own son had respected the children. Once, when a crowd was waiting for his help, his disciples wanted to push the children away. But Jesus had said, "Let the children come to me. . . ." He had shown the people that children were as important as men and women to him and to God, that sometimes grown-ups have to accept the kingdom of God as a child to enter it. How glad the mothers of the children had been!

Mary Magdalene thought, *That man who was cured of his blindness at Bethsaida, how happy he was to see again—blue sky, dusty road, laughing faces, everything that was only blackness before! But I wasn't cured of sickness. He showed me that I had done things wrong. And when he showed me the right way, I felt a new life coming to me like sight to that blind man. But now he has left us. The world looks dark again.*

The women hurried along and talked in hushed voices. "Now we are nearing the garden. Once more we will be with him. We will give him our last gift, sweet spices for his body."

"That great heavy stone is in front of the tomb. We can't move it. Will someone roll it away for us?"

The sun was rising when they came to the garden of the tomb. The sweet scent of opening flowers was on the air. Those flowers were as bright as they had been when Jesus had last visited his friend Joseph in that garden.

The women neared the tomb. Something was different than it had been when last they saw it. The stone had been rolled away. Anxious to know why, they hurried on. Mary went ahead and looked in the tomb.

"Do not be afraid," she heard a voice say. "You are looking for Jesus. He is not here. He is risen. Come and see for yourselves."

Was Jesus living? Fear, then great joy came to Jesus' mother and to Mary and Salome. "Then the sweet spices are not the last gift we can bring him?" asked Salome. But her question was a cry of joy. "If he is living, we can still see him. We *must* find him. Our whole life will not even be enough to show our love for him!"

And the three women ran toward Jerusalem to find Jesus.

Adapted from Gertrude C. Keith, "Easter Morning," *Children's Religion,* April, 1952.

Pentecost

Happy Birthday, Church!

When you go to bed at night, you know you are not alone. Mom or Dad is there to take care of you, even if you can't see them from your bedroom. They will come if you call. How good that feels!

A long time ago the followers of Jesus were afraid. They felt lonely. They did not think there was anyone to help them.

They were told to go to Jerusalem to wait for a special gift. The gift would show them what to do.

People from many lands came to Jerusalem to celebrate a holiday. It was called *Pentecost.* The followers of Jesus came, too.

They were meeting together in a room when, all of a sudden, the followers of Jesus felt something wonderful happen. The special gift was given to them. It was a strange feeling, like wind and fire. It was the Holy Spirit! They were so happy. They knew that they would never be alone again. They knew what they were going to do—tell all people about Jesus.

People could not see the Holy Spirit, but they knew the Holy Spirit was there to help them—just like you know your mom or dad is there to help you even when you can't see them.

Many people wanted to join with the followers of Jesus. They were all so happy that they wanted to share the good feeling they had. They prayed together. They learned about Jesus together. They shared their food. They shared everything. They loved each other. That is what it was like at the first church.

Adapted from *Student's Resource Book,* Living the Word, Level 4, vol. 1, no. 4 (Summer, 1979), p. 4. Used by permission of the American Baptist Board of Education and Publication.

Reformation Sunday

Here I Stand!

When most people think of the Reformation, they think first of Martin Luther, who lived about five hundred years ago in Germany.

Luther was a priest of the Roman Catholic Church and a professor at the University of Wittenberg. Martin wanted very much to live as he thought God wanted him to live. He went without food until his cheeks caved in; he confessed his sins for six hours at a time. But he soon came to see that even if he was as good as he could possibly be, he would not be good enough. He realized that it is impossible to *earn* God's favor and that what people must do is to accept God's love and forgiveness. This idea, called "justification by faith" (instead of by works), became the slogan of the Reformation.

Luther tried hard to be a good Christian. He was shocked to find that members of his church were *buying* forgiveness and privileges. Luther knew that this was not right or fair and he wrote out his ideas on parchment and nailed it to the church door on All Hallows' Eve in 1517. It was called "The Ninety-Five Theses" because he had written about ninety-five different church practices that he thought should be changed.

Soon all of Germany was talking about the ninety-five theses. One of Luther's beliefs was that the Bible, not the pope (the head of the Roman Catholic Church), is the authority for Christians. Now he was in real trouble! The church leaders were angry. They took him to court and tried to get Luther to take back his words.

"I neither can nor will take back anything," said Luther. "My conscience is chained to the Bible and I cannot go against my conscience!"

Here, the emperor interruped. He had heard enough. There was great confusion in the court. "Here I stand," said Luther. "I cannot do otherwise."

A surprising thing happened. Luther was not condemned to be burned at the stake as was the custom. Instead, after a week he was given permission to start for home.

As Luther and two friends were riding through a dark forest on their way home, a group of armed men came and kidnapped Luther. They took him to an old castle and kept him there for a year. It turned out that the kidnapping had been ordered by a friendly ruler who wanted Luther kept safe until people forgot about the trial.

It was a sad and lonely year at the castle, but Luther wrote books and pamphlets and translated the New Testament into German.

After his year in hiding he returned home to his teaching and preaching and writing.

Luther had never thought of starting a new church; but when the leaders of the old church refused to change, people who agreed with Luther began to do what they believed was right in spite of what the church said. The pastors married. They conducted services in German (the language of the people) instead of in Latin. They served the Communion wine to the people instead of having the priest drink it all.

Finally the rulers said, "This is enough. You must stop!" But by then nothing could stop the reform movement. When the reformers protested against the order that their work should go no further, they were called Protestants, and the name has stuck!

On Reformation Sunday we remember Martin Luther and other leaders of the Reformation movement that changed the course of the history of the Christian Church.

Elizabeth W. Gale

Thanksgiving

Pedro's Gift

The last of the rice had been harvested. The men had threshed it with their bare feet and the wind blew the chaff away. It had been a good year with an abundant harvest. Pedro's father loaded his sacks of rice onto the Jeepney and took them home where he stored them in large baskets, hoping to keep the rats from getting into the rice. Rice was their main food for the coming year. He set one sack of rice aside.

Pedro came running into the house, calling, "Dad, can we cut down some banana stalks to decorate the church for the Thanksgiving service tomorrow? You should see how nice it looks already. There are bunches of coconuts, stalks of sugar cane, and baskets of fruit and vegetables already on the platform."

"Sure, son," answered his dad, "choose the ones with nice

leaves, ones that the last typhoon didn't tear up."

On Thanksgiving Sunday morning Pedro's mother and other women from this church in the Philippines were up early preparing food for the dinner after church. Some of the men were barbecuing a whole pig over the open charcoal pit.

Pedro's family dressed for church. A Jeepney taxi came to get them. The family climbed in while Pedro's father loaded the sack of rice he had set aside. He called it "the Lord's rice." It was their Thanksgiving offering to God. Father turned to Pedro and asked, "Pedro, what is your offering to the Lord?"

Pedro was surprised and stammered, "Mine? Why, I didn't think I needed to bring anything. I'm just a child."

"But you have had a good year, Pedro," said his father. "God has given you good health and helped you in school, hasn't he?"

"Well, yes," Pedro replied slowly, "but what can I give God?"

"You have ten beautiful chickens, Pedro. You didn't lose even one this year," Father reminded him. Just then the driver of the Jeepney honked his horn. Pedro's father jumped in the taxi and away the family went, leaving Pedro standing by himself.

Pedro walked around to the back of their house where he kept his chickens. He looked thoughtfully at his ten white Leghorn chickens. He was proud of them. How could he give one away?

The Thanksgiving service was long but beautiful. Six babies were dedicated. The choir sang. The church was full. The missionary preached the sermon.

Then it was time for the offering when the worshipers took their gifts of money or produce to the altar. Pedro's father put the sack of rice by the Communion table. Pedro stood in the back. He carried a beautiful white chicken under his arm. He joined the others going forward. He knelt by the Communion table and placed his chicken on the floor. Then he took the piece of twine that was tied around the feet of the chicken and tied the other end to the leg of the table. He gave the best he had to God who had given so much to him.

Adapted from Harriet Houston, "Pedro's Gift," *Baptist Leader,* vol. 42, no. 8 (November, 1980), p. 6.

Universal Bible Sunday

What Is the Bible?

I have brought with me today several kinds of Bibles. I am going to give some of you one of these Bibles to read. Would you look at them and be prepared to read a little when I ask you to do so. (Bibles in Greek, Hebrew, German, Spanish, Japanese, Chinese, etc., may be given to several children.) Can you read any of these? (Response.) No, of course not; they are Bibles in different translations. (Name them.) How did you feel when you discovered you couldn't read your Bible? (If you have people in your congregation who can read a familiar verse in another language, ask them in advance to be prepared to do so at this time. The child who has the particular Bible might take it to the one who will read.) We are fortunate to have the Bible in many languages so that people from different nations around the world can read it and understand. At first the Old Testament was written in Hebrew and the New Testament in Greek, such as the copies [Jack] and [Mary] have, and only people who could read those languages could read the Bible. Today the Bible has been translated into over one thousand languages, and every year new translations are being made.

I have here one of the most interesting of all. This translation was written with dots. (Scripture cards can be obtained from the American Bible Society.) Persons who cannot see use their fingers to read the raised dots. (Read the Scripture on the card.)

What makes the Bible so important and special? (Responses.) The Bible tells us about Jesus and the story of God's work in the world. It tells us of God's love and teaches us how we are to live.

O God, we thank you for the many people who listened to you and wrote the Bible so that we might know more about your love.

William Sutterlin

Christmas

Joy to the World

(Begin this story by having a soloist or choir sing the first stanza of

"Joy to the World" to the Scottish Psalter tune "Dunfermline.")

Do you know this hymn? Of course you do. It is one of our favorite Christmas carols, "Joy to the World." _____ (the choir or soloist's name) just sang it to a different tune, one that was used about four hundred years ago!

Isaac Watts was a boy who lived in that long ago time. One Sunday after church Isaac said, "Father, I can't stand the dreary way they sing the Psalms!" His father answered that if Isaac thought he could write more fitting verses, he should try. Another story, though, tells how upset Mr. Watts would get when Isaac spoke in rhymes. Once he was going to punish him, and Isaac pleaded: "I prithee, Father, mercy take,/And I will no more verses make." The father's answer is not recorded. But Isaac did make more verses, and his father was proud of his son's creative gifts.

Isaac Watts developed those gifts thoroughly. He lectured and wrote for universities on a wide range of subjects, from the wonders of the mind to the wonders of the stars. He wrote books for children, too. And he composed six hundred hymns.

He used to read Psalm 98:4, 7, 9.

> Sing for joy to the LORD, all the earth;
>   praise him with songs and shouts of joy!. . .
> Roar, sea, and every creature in you;
>   sing, earth, and all who live on you!. . .
>   because he comes to rule the earth.
> He will rule the peoples of the world
>   with justice and fairness.

He hoped that people would remember all through the year, and all through their lives, that the Lord has come. So he thought they should sing about it, and he used these ideas to write the hymn "Joy to the World!"

People began to sing it. Some sang it and said, "What a wonderful idea, Mr. Watts, to write hymns and use words of your own." Others heard it and said, "Shame on you, Mr. Watts! Replacing the Bible with your newfangled songs!"

But people kept singing it, and years later they started to sing it at Christmas. Isaac Watts would have liked that idea very much. But then they started singing it *only* at Christmas. He would not have liked that at all.

Franklin Morgan

Bible Stories

The Bible is a treasure book of stories, some appropriate for use with children, some not. Those that appear in this section are samples of Bible stories that have been adapted for children. Before selecting a Bible story, be sure to read the section "Selecting Bible Stories with Care" on pages 52-53 and the chart titled "The Meaning of Bible Material from the View of Children of Different Ages" on pages 54-63. The sections "Techniques for Storytelling" and "Telling the Story" will also be helpful.

How God Used a Rascal

"Oh my," sighed Jacob, "I'm really afraid. I wonder what Esau will do to me tomorrow. To think that all these years I've been the winner. But tomorrow I could lose everything, even my life." Jacob had reason to be afraid. He thought, *Yeah, I'm rich now, but I got a good deal of it by cheating.*

Jacob was not too happy thinking about himself as a cheat and a rascal. "But what will Esau think of me? He is sure to remember how I cheated him. To think that I could steal from my own brother not once but twice! I'm afraid. He's sure to hate me more than ever."

Jacob shuddered. "I can still remember how angry Esau was when he found out about that second time. Was he ever angry when he discovered how I had stolen our father's final blessing!" A sad look came over Jacob's face. "So what else could I do after that? I had to run away from home. I've lived all these years in a strange land. Now it's time that my sons saw the land of their grandfather. But I sure am afraid to face Esau tomorrow."

Jacob didn't ask what had happened to Esau in twenty years.

He didn't think of what Esau looked like after twenty years. He didn't stop to wonder what Esau had been doing all those many, many years. No, all that Jacob could think of was how badly he had cheated his brother. Jacob really was afraid of what Esau would do to him the next day.

Then Jacob thought, *All right, I'll send him gifts, lots of presents. I'll send them ahead of me so that when I get there Esau won't be so angry with me.* So that is what Jacob did. After he had sent servants with many goats and many sheep ahead to Esau as presents, he sent his family ahead. Even when Jacob went off by himself on the side of the road, he couldn't really rest. He tried to sleep. The dark of night fell. Suddenly Jacob found himself fighting in the dark with a stranger. They struggled furiously. They wrestled. They fought fiercely. Jacob would not let go until the stranger had blessed him.

Later, when Jacob woke up, he knew that he was a different person than he had been before.

The day he had feared for so long came at last. He went forward calmly to meet Esau. The older twin ran to him and hugged him, saying, "Hey, it's good to see you, Jacob." Jacob replied, "Am I ever happy to see you again, Esau!" At first Esau refused the many presents Jacob had sent him. "I have plenty of sheep and goats of my own already," Esau said. Jacob insisted that Esau keep the many presents and at last Esau accepted them all.

So as the day ended, Jacob was much poorer but happier. After Jacob's wrestling in the night and his getting back together with Esau, he was no longer called just "Jacob"; people began calling him "Israel," which means "You have struggled with God and with men, and you have won." Poorer, weaker than before, but happy because his brother had forgiven him and pleased to be at home, Israel gave thanks to God.

—Based on Genesis 32

Joseph D. Ban

Daniel and the Lions

While the Hebrews lived in Babylon, the king called for some smart, handsome Hebrew young men to come to the king's home. He wanted them to learn about their new country. Daniel was one of these young men.

Daniel learned quickly and well. Before long he was made a leader. This made some of the Babylonians very jealous because they felt that one of them should have been chosen to be the leader. They tried to think of some way to get rid of Daniel. But he did his work so well that they couldn't find anything bad to tell about Daniel to the king.

Finally they thought of a trick. They knew that Daniel worshiped his God three times a day. They went to the king and said, "O king, live forever. All of us think that you should make a law that anyone who prays to a god or a man except to you, O king, for thirty days shall be put into a den of lions."

The king did not know that he was being tricked. He put his name on the paper. So the law was made: no praying to God.

Daniel heard about the new law, but he went right on praying to his God three times a day as he had always done. The Babylonians came and found him praying. They went right to the king. "O king, did you not make a law that whoever prays to anyone but you, for thirty days shall be thrown into a den of lions?"

"Yes," answered the king. "That is the new law."

"Well," the men said, "Daniel, who is one of the Hebrews, does not obey the law. He prays to his God three times a day!"

The king was very upset. He didn't want to put Daniel into a den of lions. All day long he tried to think of a way he could save Daniel.

In the evening the men went to the king again and said, "O king, you know that no law that has the king's name on it can be changed."

So the king sadly had Daniel sent to the lions. He said, "Daniel, I could not save you. May your God, whom you serve so faithfully, save you."

Daniel was put in the den of lions.

The king went to his home, the palace, but he couldn't sleep. He was worried about Daniel. As soon as it was light, he hurried to the lions' den. When he got near, he called out, "O Daniel, servant of the living God, has your God whom you serve so faithfully been able to save you from the lions?"

"O king," answered Daniel, "my God saved me. The lions have not hurt me. My God delivered me."

The king was very happy. He had Daniel taken out of the den, and he made a new law: "Worship the God of Daniel, for that God is the living God forever; God's kingdom shall always be."

—Based on Daniel 6

From *Opening the Bible,* Discovering the Bible with Children Series, Primary, vol. 2, no. 1 (September-November, 1977), pp. 58-59. © 1976 Micheal Bergamo. Used by permission of American Baptist Board of Education and Publication.

Let the Children Come

Jesus was a friendly person. He liked people. He was never too busy to spend time with anyone who came to him. He helped people who were sick. He told many stories to teach people how God wanted them to live. "God loves us," he said. "See the bright flowers and the birds flying in the air. God takes care of them. God loves you, too. You are very important to God, just as the birds and flowers are."

One day there were many people standing around Jesus asking questions and listening to what he had to say. The disciples, Jesus' helpers, were behind the crowd. "What's that noise?" whispered one of the disciples.

"I don't know. I can hardly hear what Jesus is saying," whispered another. "Look, who is coming over the hill, there, behind those rocks?" They looked and saw a group of women happily talking with one another. There were boys and girls skipping along with them. "Hey, what do they think they are doing? Why are they bringing those children here? They are going to interrupt Jesus. Of all the nerve!"

"I'll go and head them off," said one of the men. He ran toward the group of women and children. "See here, don't you see Jesus is talking with the people. You are making a lot of noise. We don't need any interruptions. Move on . . . go down the other way!"

One of the women spoke up: "We wanted the children to see and hear Jesus."

"Jesus is too busy for children! Don't you understand that? Now go away and be quiet!"

All of a sudden it did become very quiet. The happy faces of the women changed into sad faces. The children stopped their chatter. They knew they had been scolded. But Jesus, too, stopped talking. He got up and walked through the crowd. There was an angry look on his face. "Let the children come to me," he said to his disciples. "Don't turn them away! These children belong to God's kingdom.

God loves them. And I love them. Children are important! Let them be an example to you!" The disciples felt ashamed. Jesus motioned to the children to come along with him to the middle of the crowd. As the children gathered around Jesus, he put his arms around them and blessed them.

—Based on Mark 10:13-16

Arline J. Ban

Jesus Heals a Paralyzed Man

People were coming from every direction. They were going to the house where Jesus was. They heard that Jesus was teaching there.

The house was full. More people came and had to stand in the courtyard. People kept coming. They kept walking toward the house. But one man was not walking; his legs were paralyzed.

Friends who wanted to bring him to Jesus picked up his bed, called a "pallet." It was like a stretcher to carry a sick person. Each one of them got hold of a corner of the pallet and hurried to the house where Jesus was. Finally, they got to the courtyard. There were so many people that they could not get to the front door.

"Let's go around to the back," one of them said. It was hard to get through the crowds with their friend on the pallet. As they started around the house, one of the friends had an idea. "Let's go up on the roof. We could get a rope and lower our friend down into the room where Jesus is!"

The people in the house were startled when they looked up. And no wonder! The men were removing tiles to make a large hole in the roof. When they had made an opening big enough, they carefully lowered their friend on his pallet. Jesus stopped talking. He saw what had happened. He knew these friends believed he could heal their paralyzed friend. He turned to the man and said to him, "Your sins are forgiven."

Right away the man who had been paralyzed got up. He rolled up his pallet, put it under his arm, and found his friends. They danced with joy and thanked God as they all walked home.

—Based on Luke 5:17-26

Adapted from *Student's Resource Book,* Living the Word, Level 4, vol. 1, no. 2 (Winter, 1978-79), p. 38. Used by permission of the American Baptist Board of Education and Publication.

Only One Says, "Thank You"

"Unclean! Unclean!" the lepers called as they met people on the road. No one would go near lepers. They had a very bad sickness called leprosy that made ugly sores on the skin. The lepers had to live in places outside the towns so that they would not make anyone else sick.

Those who happened to get well had to be looked at and checked by the priests to be sure they were well before they could go home.

One day Jesus walked on the road between Samaria and Galilee. Near a small town he heard, "Unclean! Unclean!" Jesus saw ten men who were sick with leprosy.

"Jesus," they called, "help us, please." They thought Jesus might give them some money. Jesus wanted to help. He looked at them and said, "Go to the priests. Let them see that you are well. Then you can go back to live with your families."

The ten men were surprised, but they started to town to find the priest. At first they could not see that they were changing; but each one got better as he walked. Their sores healed. Their skin got smooth and clean again.

"We are getting well!" they said to one another.

"Jesus did it for us!" they said.

"Hurry, let's find the priest."

They walked faster and faster down the road. Suddenly one stopped.

"I'm going back to find Jesus," he called. The others hurried on to town, but he turned around. He ran fast.

"Jesus! Jesus! Praise God! You made me well. I had to find you and thank you." He was so thankful he fell on his face at Jesus' feet.

Jesus stopped. "Ten men were healed. Where are the others? Why are you the only one to come back to thank God?"

"I don't know. I only know I had to thank the one who made me well," the man said.

"I'm glad you came," Jesus said. "Get up and go to the priest now. Your faith has made you well."

—Based on Luke 17:11-19

From *Opening the Bible,* Discovering the Bible with Children Series, Primary, vol. 3, no. 2 (December, 1978-February, 1979), pp. 48-49. © 1978 Micheal Bergamo. Used by permission of the American Baptist Board of Education and Publication.

To Be Great

Jesus and his disciples were on their way to Jerusalem. Jesus walked ahead of the others. The disciples were worried and afraid of what would happen when they got to Jerusalem.

Disciples James and John were brothers. They suddenly began to walk faster than the others. They wanted to catch up with Jesus because they had an important question to ask him.

"Teacher," they said when they reached him, "there is something we want you to do for us."

"What is it?" Jesus asked them. "What do you want me to do for you?"

"When you are the ruler of God's future kingdom, we want to be the most important people under you," answered James and John. "Let one of us sit at your right and the other at your left."

Jesus shook his head slowly. "You don't know what you are asking for," he said. "Are you able to suffer with me? Are you ready to go with me through all the dangers ahead? Are you willing to die with me?"

"Yes, we can! We will!" James and John answered quickly. James and John were sure they could do all that Jesus expected, but they did not know all the problems that were ahead.

"I'm sure you want to give your lives to God," Jesus said, "but I cannot grant your wish to have the most important places. It is God who will decide who is truly great."

By now the other ten disciples had caught up with Jesus and James and John. When they heard that James and John had asked Jesus for the best positions for themselves, the disciples were very angry. Jesus stopped walking. He called the twelve men to come together around him.

"You know," Jesus said, "our rulers have the power to tell people what they can or cannot do. Often they are cruel and unfair. This is not God's way. If one of you wants to be great, he must be a servant to the others. In fact, the one who wants to be first must be a slave of everyone. God sent me not to be served and treated like a king but to give my life in helping and serving others. That's what it means to be truly great."

—Based on Mark 10:33-37

Elizabeth W. Gale

The Rich Man

Joseph, a rich young man, heard that Jesus was teaching near his village. His mother and little sisters had left their house and had gone to try to find the teacher. Joseph thought he would like to see Jesus, too. Jesus was just leaving as Joseph came near.

"Good teacher," said Joseph, "What shall I do to inherit eternal life?" Jesus looked at him and said, "Why do you ask? Follow the law. You know what that is."

Joseph was impatient. "I have followed the law from the time I was a tiny baby. I want to know what I lack to be part of God's kingdom and live forever."

Jesus said to him, "You are asking me because you are selfish. Think first of what you can do to make other people happy, and then you will be ready for God's kingdom. Give away your money. You have lived for many years and had every luxury while the poor and needy and lame have starved and sometimes died. Divide your luxuries. Don't be selfish any more. Take some of the uncomfortable things which other people have to endure. You will not have such a soft bed, but you will be part of God's kingdom. It is worse to be selfish than to disobey the written rules."

Joseph went away disappointed and very sad. He thought Jesus would tell him he was good enough or suggest some simple thing to do. This doing away with the things he had bought for his own enjoyment seemed impossible. He thought he never could do that.

—Based on Matthew 19:16-22

Written by a grade 5 church school class.

The Church

For Communion Sunday

Does your family have a book of family pictures? Would anybody like to tell us about one picture in your book? (Give several children a chance to respond briefly.) Pictures help us remember people and things that happened in the past.

Here is a picture of my family. (Tell anything special about it.) Every time I look at this picture, I think of my family and the time we. . . (finish the sentence if the picture is related to an event). It reminds me of how much I love the people in my family and how much they love me.

When Jesus lived on earth there were no cameras; so there are no photographs of him. Of course we have many pictures that people have drawn to show how they imagine Jesus might have looked. But Jesus himself thought of a way for his friends to remember him.

On the night before he died, he had supper with his friends. He took from the table some of the bread and wine, and he said, "Whenever you eat this bread and drink this cup, think of me. Remember how much I love you."

On this Sunday (and whenever your church observes Communion) people in our church eat a piece of bread and drink some wine (or grape juice). We do this to remember Jesus, to think about how much he loves us, and to show by this act that we love him and try to live as he taught.

Mary Dunlop

Presentation of Bibles to Children

Today is a very special time for us because all the boys and girls going into grade ____ will receive their very own Bible as a gift from the people of _____ (name of the church).

(Holding up a Bible, show the presentation page.) What do you see? (Accept any answers.) _____ saw his name. That's because this Bible is addressed to him.

While I was writing each of your names in these Bibles yesterday, the mail carrier handed me a letter. I thought, "On Sunday I'll be like a mail carrier as I deliver this book of messages to the boys and girls." These Bibles have your names on them just as my letter does.

I have my letter here. (Show unopened letter.) You can see that it has not been opened. I'll never know what's in it until I open it. So it is with your Bible. You will never know what messages or news for you are in it until you open it and read it.

Your Bible addressed to you and my letter addressed to me are alike in that they both contain news and messages we will never know until we open and read what's inside. My letter and your Bible are also different. My letter was written a few days ago; your Bible was written a long, long time ago. My letter is written in easy words that I know and understand. Your Bible is written differently from the way you talk and, therefore, is sometimes hard to understand. My letter is short, only a few pages. Your Bible is long. It contains poems, stories, history, and several letters.

I can begin at the beginning and read my letter straight through in a very short time. The best way to read your Bible is to select certain parts and read those first. We have therefore placed bookmarks in several places in your Bible where you will find stories you have heard and perhaps some poetry you have memorized.

Once I have read my letter, I will put it aside until I answer it. Then I will throw it away. But I will keep reading my Bible as long as I live.

Most us need help in learning to use and understand the Bible. Parents and teachers and our pastor can help, but you will have to work at it, too.

This afternoon I'm going to open my letter and read it. I don't usually keep a letter a whole day without opening it! I wonder what my letter will tell me!

I am happy to give you, on behalf of your church, your very own Bibles. (Mention each child's name as the Bible is given to him or her.) I hope you will open your Bible this afternoon and find some message in it for you.

Grace B. Harger

The Church Is People

"Church" is a word that has several different meanings. When we say, "I'm going to church," do we mean we're going to the church building or do we mean we're going to worship or do we mean we're going to be with other members of this particular church group?

The building is not really the church. The church is people, many kinds of people who gather to worship God and who go out to do God's work in the world.

All of us are needed to help this community of people be a worshiping, serving church. People do different things to help us worship and serve. As I mention each task, let's ask all the people who do that task to stand until we're finished with our time together: call on the sick, teach in the church school, deliver meals on wheels, sing in the choir, serve on a board or committee, pray for the church, worship with the other members (name as many tasks as you wish that describe people in your congregation).

Now that everyone is standing, will you children go and stand with your families or with some other adult? Let's all hold hands, raise our joined hands, and shout, "The church is people!" (Or you might have the congregation sing the first stanza and refrain of "We Are the Church" by Avery and Marsh, if it is familiar.)

Adapted from material contributed by Mary Dunlop.

We Need One Another

On sheets of light-colored paper (one for each child) draw an eye, an ear, a hand, or a foot (one on each piece of paper) in advance.

Give each child one of the papers. Ask all those who have a picture of an eye to go to one section of the congregation, the ears to another, the hands to another, and the feet to another. Ask the children to face the people in their section and to hold up their signs so that the people can see them.

"The church is like the body. It has many parts. Will all parts of the body please stand?" (Everyone stands.)

"If the foot said, 'I am not a part of the body because I'm not a hand' (foot section sits), it would still be a part of the body; but how would the body walk?

"If the ear said, 'I am not a part of the body because I'm not an eye' (ear section sits), it would still be a part of the body; but how would the body hear?

"If the hand said, 'I am not a part of the body because I'm not a foot' (hand section sits), it would still be part of the body; but how would the body write or be fed?

"If the eye said, 'I am not a part of the body because I am not an ear' (eye section sits), it would still be a part of the body; but how would the body see?

"But God made us so that we need all our parts in order to do all the things that the body can do. What a strange thing it would be if the whole body were an ear!" (Ear section stands.)

"No, all of us together are part of the body that is the church (other sections stand) and we all need one another!"

—Based on 1 Corinthians 12:12-26

Adapted from material contributed by Robert Walk.

The Mission Outreach of the Church

Deaf, but Not Dumb

Susanne Powers, a missionary teacher in the Christian school in Balasore, India, heard that the state of Orissa, in India, was to have a program for deaf children in a few schools. "If there is a program for deaf children, we must have it here in Balasore," she said to herself and she began to pray about it.

One day when she was visiting in a village, a father stopped her and said, "Please take my daughter to study in your school." But Miss Powers replied, "I won't take your daughter, but I will take your son."

"What?" the father answerd. "He is deaf and dumb! He'll become a beggar." Many people in India think that deaf people are naturally dumb and not able to speak or to learn. Deaf children are considered to be dull and useless, a burden on their families. In fact, sometimes neighbors do not even know there is a deaf child because the parents believe that the child's deafness is something to hide.

The boy's father allowed his deaf son to go to Balasore with Miss Powers and she began to find ways to teach him. She went to the government office to get permission to start a class for deaf children but found to her surprise that the government's program was to put the deaf children in the same classes with hearing children. Sue Powers was shocked. "These deaf children don't know how to speak," she began. "They can't hear and they don't know how to read lips. The teachers already have 50 to 60 children in their classes! It wouldn't help the children and it would be a burden to the teachers if the deaf children were put in the regular classes!"

Sue Powers knew now that if the deaf children were to be educated, she would have to start a school for them. The first morning 11 children and their parents joined in the opening worship service. A year later there were 25 deaf children and 3 teachers and a helper. For part of the school day the deaf children attend classes with the hearing children and the other part of the day the deaf children are in their own classes with their special teachers.

Sue Powers and an Indian teacher wrote a book about their school for the deaf. It is called *Deaf, but Not Dumb*. Government officials were impressed by what they read. They went to Balasore and visited the Christian school and liked what they saw. One of the government people said, "Miss Powers, why work only in Balasore? You can come and help us in other places, too!"

"Isn't it wonderful how God works!" thought Sue Powers. "The state is now adopting the program that we developed. We trust that as this work grows, many deaf children will become speaking, educated, useful citizens of India and that they will come to know Jesus Christ in whose name the work was started."

Adapted from Eileen R. James, "Mission Matters," *Baptist Leader,* vol, 42, no. 12 (March, 1981), pp. 6-7. Used by permission of the American Baptist Board of Education and Publication.

A Dime That Multiplied and Traveled

Robert Rodriguez lives in Manhattan, Kansas, where he works at the American Institute of Baking. In 1979 he was sent to Venezuela in South America to teach some courses on baking to the people there. While he was in Venezuela he visited a family with a nine-year-old daughter named Anita. Robert became her "tio" or pretend uncle.

After Robert returned to his home in Kansas, he received a letter from Anita. With the letter was a dime that Anita asked Robert to give to the·nearest church.

The First Baptist Church was the nearest church; so Robert Rodriguez took the dime to the church office and told the secretary where it had come from. He was embarrassed at the size of the amount. "I thought they would laugh me out of the place," he said, but he knew that to Anita ten cents was a lot of money.

The church secretary recognized what a special gift this was and decided that the dime should be used for something special. When other people heard about Anita's sacrificial gift, they began to give money to the church. One person said, "Sometimes our world is so shaken by problems that we grow weary. And then a beautiful story of a little girl in Venezuela . . . that gift, like a candle shining in the darkness, touched us and made us humble." He gave a hundred dollars.

The church decided to use Anita's dime and all the money which came because of her gift, to provide scholarships for students in Cap Haitien, Haiti.

From a child in Venezuela, to Kansas, to Haiti, Anita's dime traveled. What stories it could tell!

Adapted from "It Started with a Dime," *The American Baptist Magazine,* vol. 178, no. 5 (May, 1980), p. 23.

Chitta Babu

Chitta Babu lives in Bangladesh. He had to drop out of school after the eighth grade to help support his family. In time he became a mailman and was sent to Jamalpur. Although he had little education, his honest, hard work and his good mind gained him advancements. When he was offered better jobs that would have taken him to other places, he turned them down because he believed that God had called him to Jamalpur to start a church there.

After ten years in Jamalpur, Chitta Babu married a Christian woman from a nearby town. Together they became a Christian family and have four daughters and one son. Mrs. Babu became a teacher.

Most of the time Chitta Babu and his family were the only Christians in Jamalpur. Sometimes a Christian government worker would be sent to Jamalpur but never stayed very long. Chitta Babu invited friends, neighbors, and even strangers to his home to sing Christian songs and to talk about Jesus and his teachings. He talked about his faith with anyone, even the highest government official. Although some people were interested in Jesus, the fear of losing their jobs or of being rejected by their family and community kept them from becoming Christians.

But Chitta Babu never .gave up his dream of a church in Jamalpur. He put a cross on the outside wall of his home to tell everyone who passed by that here lived a follower of Jesus.

Twenty-five years after Chitta Babu first went to Jamalpur, he began to see his dream come true when a missionary came to help.

Chitta Babu helped the missionary. After work he would pedal his bicycle as far as twenty miles to visit people who wanted to know about Jesus. Or he would ride on the motorcycle behind the missionary. Mrs. Babu would often spend her only day off to teach new Christians.

Now there is a group of Christians in Jamalpur that will soon become a real church. Chitta feels that this never would have happened without the partnership of missionaries.

Adapted from Eileen R. James, "Mission Matters," *Baptist Leader,* vol. 42, no. 11 (February, 1981), pp. 10-11. Used by permission of the American Baptist Board of Education and Publication.

People Who Have Made a Difference

A Woman and a Bus

Did you ever think that a woman could use a bus to teach people about God's love? I bet you never thought of it quite like that!

Not too many years ago it was against the law in many places for black people and white people to sit together on a public bus. The black people could sit only in the back half of the bus and the white people could sit in the front. But if there were not enough seats, the black people had to stand and let the white people sit.

Although that was the way things had been done for many years, it wasn't fair. Black people knew that God loves everyone; so why shouldn't everyone have a fair chance to sit on the bus?

One day Mrs. Rosa Parks got on a bus. She was very tired. She did what she was not supposed to do. She sat down in the section for whites only. When the bus driver came to tell her that she had to move and give up her seat, she decided not to do it. That was a brave thing to do. She knew that she could be punished. But she also knew that the rule was not fair.

Many other black people found out what she did and they all decided not to ride the buses again until the rule was changed.

Since that day when Mrs. Parks bravely kept her seat, both black and white people have learned more about showing God's love by the way we treat other people.

Virginia Sargent

A Migrant with Hope

Elizabeth Loza Newby was raised in a family of migrant farm

workers. Until the age of fourteen, she slept with the rest of her family in the back of a pick-up truck because her mother felt that it was cleaner than the farm camps. In the camps one family, no matter how large, was given one room. Often there was no electricity or running water but there were rats!

The Loza family went from the cotton fields of Texas to the sugar beets in Kansas, the cherry crops in Michigan, the avocado, lettuce, and grape crops in California, and back to the Texas cotton fields again.

The Loza family, like other migrant people, was trapped in this kind of cycle and many children at an early age often gave up any dreams of another life.

The Spanish-speaking migrant children were often placed in classes for retarded children or were just ignored because of their problems with the language. School was very difficult for these children because they moved so often and their parents did not encourage them in school. Often the children worked in the fields to help make the family's living even though it was against the law for children to work.

Elizabeth and her friends were always placed at the back of the classroom, the cafeteria, and the bus because they were different. Finally Elizabeth rebelled. She studied hard and refused to get married at age fifteen.

Her junior high and senior high teachers were so impressed with her work and her ability that they raised money to help her go to college.

Elizabeth Loza is now married to a minister and they have a daughter. Mrs. Newby speaks to groups across the country to try to help improve the terrible conditions for the two million migrant farm workers in America today.

Adapted from an article in *The Philadelphia Bulletin*, May 3, 1980. Reprinted by permission of *The Philadelphia Bulletin*.

Twentieth-Century Prophet

One of the great Christians of the last century was Walter Rauschenbusch. He was born in Rochester, New York, seven years after his parents came to the United States from Germany.

When he was a boy he tried to earn some money by working during the summers on a farm in Pennsylvania. He worked from four-thirty in the morning until eight o'clock at night—a long, hard day. How much do you suppose he earned for such a long day's work? Twenty-five cents, plus his food!

Growing into manhood was not easy for Walter. One day when he was seventeen, he prayed hard, asking God to help him. He experienced a deep, loving, mysterious response from God. As a result of that experience, Walter gave his life to God and decided to become a minister.

His first church was a small, poor German congregation in the slums of New York City. He worked there for eleven years. He saw how poor the people were and how they suffered from not having enough to eat, from living in crowded apartments, and from not having proper medical care. The thing that hurt him most was the number of little children who died.

Walter joined with other community leaders in trying to get playgrounds for children, better housing for families, and jobs for those who needed them.

At this time in his life he had another powerful experience that changed his life. It happened while Walter was attending a big meeting in New York at which a Catholic priest spoke. When the priest said the words from the Lord's Prayer, " . . . Thy kingdom come, Thy will be done, on earth as it is in heaven," members of the crowd sprang to their feet and cheered. The priest went on to say that all people are children of God and brothers and sisters to one another. He said that poverty and suffering are against God's will.

This experience led Walter to a deeper study of the Bible. He discovered that the gospel of Jesus is not only for individual people but also for the laws and customs that allow some people to be very rich while many others are very poor. He worked so hard in helping the poor that he became ill with a sickness that left him with deafness for the rest of his life.

Being deaf did not stop Walter Rauschenbusch from working for the poor! As a professor at Rochester Theological Seminary he taught many young people. He lectured and preached. He wrote books. His message was always the same—the church must work to make the kingdom of God a reality.

Every time we say " . . . Thy kingdom come, Thy will be done, on earth as it is in heaven," we join with Walter Rauschenbusch in praying for changes that will bring the good life—decent housing, enough food, fair jobs, and peace—to all people everywhere.

Elizabeth W. Gale

Evil Repaid with Goodness

Charles Journeycake was an Indian of the Leni-Lenape tribe. His people were known as the most peace-loving and religious of the Algonquian tribes. Many of them were Christians. When the white settlers came, these Indians were willing to share their lands with them and continued to be their friends. Many of the Leni-Lenapes supported the white struggle for independence.

After the American Revolution the new government that these Indians had helped to bring into being told them that their land was needed by the white settlers. The Indians were promised that if they would go to Ohio their lands would be theirs forever and that if they would take into their villages and farms some of the smaller tribes, they would be allowed to have a representative in the new Congress.

So off to Ohio they went. They built villages with churches and cleared the land for farms. But then trouble came. Other Indians thought the Leni-Lenapes were too friendly with the white people, and the white people wanted the Indians' land. The Leni-Lenapes were taken to northern Ohio as hostages. Weeks later when they got back to their farms the white people borrowed their knives, hoes, and everything that might be used as weapons. Then the whites killed all but a few of the Indians—men, women, and children.

The few who escaped joined other Indians who had never heard of the Christian faith. For fifty years these Indians wanted nothing to do with white people or Christianity.

Once again the United States government told the Indians that they had to leave Ohio and go to a new Indian territory beyond Missouri. It took two years for them to make the trip. Charles Journeycake was ten years old when they arrived. The rivers were flooding, but young Charles plunged through the water and led the horses across. On the shore was a young missionary who had just arrived in that wild country. Charles and the missionary became friends. Six years later Charles was baptized and a few years afterward his parents were also baptized.

Charles was a hunter and traveled far and wide. He could speak four different Indian languages and as he traveled on the Great Plains, wherever he found a gathering of Indians he spoke to them about Jesus.

Charles was a leader and in his later years was an ordained minister. When his people were moved again, this time to Oklahoma, he went with them and established churches in the new territory. He was one of the first trustees of Bacone College—a school for Indian students.

Charles said, "We have been broken up and moved six times. . . . We thought when we had moved across the Missouri River and paid for our homes in Kansas we were safe. But in a few years the white man wanted our country. We had good farms, built comfortable houses and big barns. We had good schools for our children and listened to the same gospel the white man listens to. The white man came in from Missouri and drove our cattle and horses away, and if our people followed them they were killed. We try to forget these things, but we would not forget that the white man brought us the blessed gospel of Christ, the Christian's hope. This more than pays for all we have suffered."

Charles Journeycake practices Jesus' teaching about forgiveness. He is to be remembered as an outstanding Christian leader.

But that is not the end of the story! Not only did Charles Journeycake and his Indian people forgive the whites for their mistreatment, but they also did what the New Testament teaches—"If someone has done you wrong, do not repay him with a wrong. Try to do what everyone considers to be good" (Romans 12:17, TEV).

When Central Baptist Seminary was preparing to open in Kansas City, the seminary did not have a shelf or a book! Guess who gave money to the seminary for books—the granddaughter of Charles Journeycake and other Indians! And later these same Indians sold some of their land so that the seminary could erect a library building.

I'm sorry about the way Indian Americans have been treated in the past, and I'm grateful for Indian Christians like Charles Journeycake who could forgive those who treated them so unfairly. How about you?

Adapted from an article that appeared in *Central Region Life,* published by the Central Region of the American Baptist Churches in the U.S.A., Topeka, Kansas.

Home and Family

It's Okay to Make Mistakes

Linda's school books fell off her bike just as she turned the corner. *Oh, how lucky! They just missed that puddle!* She jumped off her bike quickly and scooped up the books into her school bag. *Mr. Williams would really be mad at me for getting his science book muddy. Why did I stay and watch the game? It is so late! Now I have to hurry. I have to get those newspapers delivered on time. Today's my big chance!* she thought. *I'll prove to my brother Steve that I am old enough to have a paper route. I'll show him that girls are really good at delivering papers!*

It didn't take Linda long to check in at home and be on her way. She counted the names on the list and the number of papers she had to deliver, just as Steve had told her to. Then she balanced the papers carefully on her bike. *I don't want these to fall, that is for sure.* She liked her new job. *This isn't hard at all!* she thought. But when she got to the end of the list she still had three papers left. *Oh, I made a mistake! How could I?* Linda felt awful! *Who did I miss? How will I ever know?* The more she thought about it, the worse she felt. *What can I do? I could just forget about those extra papers and wait to see if anyone calls and complains.* That idea didn't make her feel any better. *Why did I make a mistake? On my first day, too!*

It was getting later in the day. Linda looked down the street and saw her father coming home from work. "Hi, Linda, why the worried look?"

Linda told him what had happened. "People will be mad at me because I didn't deliver their paper. Steve will think I am not able to take over his route."

"Come on," said her father. "It's okay to make mistakes. Let's see what we can do to make it right. We can take the list and go back

111

to each place on your route. Maybe you will remember the places you missed. And if you can't remember, we will just ask people if they have their papers."

Linda felt that she had failed. She had wanted to do it right the first time. But then she went back with her father to check each house on the list. They made it into a game, a sort of mystery.

"What are the clues to the missing places?" laughed Father.

"Who is missing a paper?" laughed Linda as they checked off the houses on her list. In no time at all they found where the papers belonged.

At supper time Steve asked: "Well, did you get the papers delivered okay?"

"No," said Linda, "I made some mistakes the first time, but I figured it out all right." Linda turned to her dad and they both winked at each other.

Arline J. Ban

Forgiveness for Rick

"Don't forget to come home at eleven o'clock," Rick's mother said. "You have to take care of Robbie so that I can work at our church bake sale."

"I won't forget, I promise," Rick yelled. He jumped on his bike and rode off to meet Mike.

"Let's race," Mike said. "We want to be the first ones at the beach."

Soon they were busy collecting shells on the sand.

"Hey! What's that red thing over in the grass?" asked Rick. Both boys ran toward it at once.

"It's a kite, but it's torn," said Mike. "Let's fix it."

At Mike's house they worked on the kite. All at once Rick looked at the clock. "Oh no!! I forgot!" he cried out. And he dropped the kite and ran home.

"Where have you been?" his mother asked. "I had to find someone to take my place at the sale because of you. Go to your room until supper."

A little while before supper time, his mother came through the door. Before Rick could say anything, his mother leaned over and kissed him gently. She said, "You knew it was wrong to break your promise. But I forgive you. I do not want us to be angry at each other any more. I will give you another chance. Will you stay with Robbie a few minutes after we eat? The new neighbors want to ask me something."

Rick gave his mother a big hug. All he could think to say was "Thanks, Mom, thanks."

Adapted from *Opening the Bible,* Discovering the Bible with Children Series, Primary, vol. 3, no. 4 (June-August, 1979), p. 21. Used by permission of the American Baptist Board of Education and Publication.

Different but Still Friends

Ben could now grin from ear to ear because people at the Little League field smiled when they saw him. He had not been grinning a few weeks ago, because he was such a terrible ball player. The manager had moved him from first base to shortstop, then from shortstop to catcher. Ben had even tried pitching, but the closest he could throw the ball to the bat was at the batter's ankle.

Ben's grin had begun to replace the fixed frown on his face when Bill, his true friend, had said, "Ben, why don't you hang up the bat and pick up the pencil?"

"What do you mean?" Ben had asked.

"We need somebody to write to our city newspaper and ask them to help us get uniforms. You are the only one on the team who can spell and say things that sound right. The manager knows baseball upside down, and he spells it that way, too. So-o-o, come on, Ben!" Bill kept begging Ben to do it.

"Bill, I'm going to try. Guess it won't hurt," said Ben.

Ben began to write. He wrote about the beginning of the team, batting averages, names of players, wins and losses of the team. He thanked the people for the new uniforms. Ben's letter let everybody know about the team. The newspaper company asked Ben to write about the team every week.

Ben was happy because he was doing what he could do well. The other members of the team were pleased to read about themselves in the newspaper. The people in the town enjoyed reading about the games. The plan was good for everyone!

That's what happens when we each use the gifts God has given us for the good of all.

Adapted from *Primary Workbook,* Uniform Series, vol. 6, no. 4 (June-August, 1975), p. 43. Used by permission of the American Baptist Board of Education and Publication.

The Littlest McGee

Tad had the longest name in the family. Thaddeus Sullivan Angus McGee. But he himself was the littlest of all the McGees.

First came Papa, who was six feet four. Next came Mama, who reached to Papa's chin. Then came Robert and Tessie and then the seven-year-old twins, Marty and Mary, who were large for their age. Last of all came Tad, who was four and small for his age.

"He's even small for his size!" teased Marty.

Tad didn't think this was funny—not one bit. He was tired of being the littlest McGee. He knew his family loved him, but every time he wanted to do something interesting or important, someone was sure to say, "No, Tad, you're too little."

Take this very Saturday. Papa and Robert had already left for a fishing trip. Tessie was invited to spend the day with friends. The twins were getting ready for their church school picnic.

"I want to go, too!" Tad had cried as each plan was announced. Each time somebody had said, "No, Tad, you're too little."

It was a long, lonesome day. Mama had expected to work in the garden, with Tad playing beside her. But as they started outdoors, the phone rang.

"Well," said Mama excitedly as she put down the receiver, "that was Mrs. Branson. She and Mr. Branson and Jimmy are driving through here today. They'll be with us for dinner. So I'll have to do some housecleaning and marketing instead of working in the garden."

Tad played by himself outdoors for a while. Then he went indoors and looked at picture books. He stood at the window and watched the cars go by. He felt very, very small.

In the afternoon Mama said, "Now we'll go to the store." She picked up her purse and her car keys and her shopping list. She turned the bolt on the back door. She snapped the spring lock on the front door. Tad climbed into the car beside her, and off they went. They got the groceries and went to the drugstore. It was 4:30 when they got home. Mama looked in her purse for the house key.

"I guess I didn't bring it with me. Oh, dear!" She looked again. She looked in all her pockets. No key. "Maybe I forgot to lock the front door," she said hopefully, hurrying up the steps. But she hadn't forgotten.

"You locked the back door, too, Mama," said Tad. "I watched you."

"Oh, dear." Mama sounded worried. "I have to get into the

kitchen and start dinner right away or I'll never be ready in time for the Bransons."

She started walking around the house, looking to see if any of the windows were open. But the only window open was the bathroom window. It was raised about eight inches from the bottom. The McGees had left it open because it was stuck. It wouldn't go up, and it wouldn't go down.

Tad pointed to it, but Mama shook her head. "I couldn't squeeze through that little opening."

"I could," said Tad.

"But honey, you're too—" Mama had been about to say "You're too little," but she stopped. For once, being little was better than being big. "All right," she said. "You try."

Mama got the screwdriver from the garage and pried loose the screen. She picked Tad up and boosted him high enough to reach the window.

He put his head in first. Then he wriggled and squirmed until he could reach the dressing table below the window. The rest of him came tumbling after. He swiveled around on his stomach, let his legs go over the side, and dropped to the floor. He ran to the front hall. He stretched way up and put both hands on the doorknob and twisted it hard. The door opened.

"Hey, Mama! Now you can come in!"

When the Bransons arrived and the rest of the McGees came home, dinner was ready. But before anyone sat down at the table, Mama told everybody how Tad had opened the front door. "It's a good thing Tad was with me. Who else in the family is the right size to get through that window?"

Tad could see that she was very proud of him. Robert and Tessie and the Bransons said "Oh!" and "Ah!" Even the twins stared at him with admiration.

Papa smiled down at him. "So you see, Thaddeus Sullivan Angus McGee, whether you're big or little, you're always just the right size for something."

Tad grinned back at Papa. Tonight even the littlest McGee felt big.

Adapted from Dorothy Ballard, "The Littlest McGee," *Presbyterian Life*, May 1, 1962. This story is copyrighted by *Presbyterian Life*.

Personal Experiences of the Storyteller

A personal experience of an individual is authentic and helpful when told by the one who had the experience, but it may lose its meaning when told by someone else. The story "Joy Is a Piece of Hard Candy" is printed here not to be retold, but as an example of the way a meaningful personal experience may be shared.

Joy Is a Piece of Hard Candy

As a teenager I learned a song at church camp. The first line went like this: "I've got the joy, joy, joy, joy down in my heart." When I sang that song I always wondered what it meant to feel joy. I knew what happy meant but did not quite know what joy was.

During the summer after my first year in seminary I had an experience that helped me know what real joy is.

I was on my way to Glacier National Park in Montana to be a national park chaplain. I had arrived in Chicago on a train that was forty-five minutes late. I was upset and worried that I might miss my connecting train to Montana. My hands began to sweat and I got very nervous.

I got in a taxi and told the driver my problem and where I needed to go. As we pulled away from the curb, he put a piece of hard candy through an opening in the bullet-proof partition and said, "Here, this is for you. Now sit back and relax and I'll get you to your train as soon as I possibly can." This comment and act of kindness came at a time when the newspapers were full of stories about taxi drivers being shot and the special bullet-proof shields being put in the cars.

I could not believe what I was experiencing. I did not know how to respond. As I unwrapped that piece of red, cinnamon-flavored candy, I thought, *This man is not an ordinary cabdriver. Something is special about him.*

I asked, "Do you give candy to all your passengers?"

"Yup," he replied, "that's the best hard candy I could buy. The way I see it, almost everybody in this city is rushed. Most of the time that makes us uptight and crabby. So when customers get into my cab, I like to add a little joy to their day."

By this time I was beginning to wonder what made this man do this unusual thing. He remarked, "I am a *rich man,* but some people don't realize it." As we rode towards the station he told me about his life and his family. He had been saved from death in World War II by a friend. His son had one time been arrested for drug dealing but was now a certified public accountant. He also told me about his wife who loved him even after thirty-five years of married life. "These people," he remarked, "have given me a lot of joy, love, and contentment. That's why I am so rich. It doesn't cost me anything to give some of it away."

As I got out of the cab, paid my fare, and hurried to my train, I realized that I had been given more than just a piece of hard candy. This cabdriver had received love in his life that produced joy in his heart. He, in turn, wanted to give joy to others.

Donald Harrington

Current News

News items from current newspapers or magazines, or from radio or television, may sometimes provide good sources for story ideas. The sample that follows might be used to show the influence of one person in bringing about a change in unjust social conditions. Or it could portray the results of injustice in the lives of children. Read the section on "Tips for Writing Your Own Story" on page 68.

Del. woman's request began a long struggle for school integration

By Sharon Sexton
Special to The Inquirer

WILMINGTON—The yellow school bus drove up the dirt lane in front of Sarah Bulah's chicken farm each morning, kicking up dust in dry weather, splashing mud when it rained.

Every afternoon, the bus bumped back down the lane, carrying the children home.

"I kept seeing this bus dropping off children all along the way, and I thought, 'My, that's funny,'" Mrs. Bulah recalled last week. It seemed funny because Mrs. Bulah drove the family automobile up and down the same lane each day, taking her daughter, Shirley, to and from school. The bus never stopped at the Bulah farm.

"One day, when it snowed and I was afraid to drive Shirley, her daddy said he couldn't see why the state couldn't give Shirley bus transportation like the other children.

"So, I said to myself, you don't know until you ask."

What Sarah Bulah asked for was, back in 1951, unthinkable—so unthinkable that it set off a public debate that continues today.

Mrs. Bulah is black; her daughter is black. The children that rode the yellow school bus every morning were white, and they were on their way to an all-white school separated by several farms from the black elementary school Shirley attended.

Mrs. Bulah's simple request that the bus drop Shirley at the road that led to her one-room black school forced the integration of Delaware's public schools and evolved into a desegregation battle that will be fought again this week in federal court here.

Beginning Wednesday, U.S. District Judge Murray M. Schwartz will preside over the trial of the state's plan to divide into four smaller districts the New Castle County School District he created in a 1978 desegregation order.

When Mrs. Bulah made her request 30 years ago, a white resident warned that "blood would flow like water" in the streets of their rural Hockessin neighborhood. Blood never flowed, but lawsuits did and legislation and epithets did, too.

A lot has happened to Mrs. Bulah, too, since she first asked the bus driver to stop at her farm. Mrs. Bulah's husband, Fred, has died. Shirley is married and has a child of her own. The chicken farm has been sold, and Mrs. Bulah lives alone in an immaculate Wilmington apartment with rows of leafy potted plants and walls decorated with family photographs.

She is 83 now, and cataracts have ruined her eyes; but in a soft voice reminiscent of the South Carolina farm where she grew up, she remembers the struggle in precise detail.

"It was a one-room school," Mrs. Bulah said of Hockessin School No. 107, the black elementary school. "One room and one teacher. And no running water. The children drank from a 10-gallon jug with water that had been sitting there for days. Dry toilets."

By the time Shirley entered the third grade, she could not write the letter "B" properly.

"Two years in that school and she couldn't make a straight "B." It wasn't the teacher's fault. She had 20 to 25 children, all different ages, in the same room. She couldn't do justice to them."

"Shirley's desk had one leg and one leg on a building block. One leg was on a building block, a four-by-eight building block."

The state board of education had responded to Mrs. Bulah's initial request by citing the state law which forbade white and black children to ride on the same bus. The board also informed her that there was no appropriation for a bus for the black school.

Louis Redding, the Wilmington lawyer recommended to the Bulah family by a black minister, told the state that if there was no bus for the black school, Shirley would be admitted to Hockessin School No. 29, the four-room, four-teacher, white school with the grassy playground, the combination auditorium-gymnasium and, of course, the bus.

The school system responded to that request by sprucing up the black school with plumbing, new desks and new hardwood floors that Mrs. Bulah said "shined like glass."

But the attention came too late. The case was already before Chancellor Collins Seitz of the Court of Chancery.

In 1951, the law permitted separate schools for white and blacks as long as the schools were equal. However, Seitz ruled in April, 1952, that because the facilities of school No. 29 and school No. 107 were not equal, No. 29 would have to admit black children.

That decision was upheld by the Delaware Supreme Court in August and, one week later, Mrs. Bulah drove her daughter to Hockessin School No. 29.

Reprinted by permission of *The Philadelphia Inquirer,* February 1, 1981.

Using an Object

Properly used, objects are effective in focusing attention. Excessively or improperly used, they may detract from the story's message. Be sure to read the section "Using an Object," which begins on page 25.

Bees and Flowers

(If possible, obtain a honeycomb from a beekeeper, fruit stand, or farmer's market for use with this story. If this is not possible, use a good picture of a honeycomb.)

This is a honeycomb. The beekeeper puts wooden frames like this into the beehive. The female bees do all the rest of the work in a bee colony. They make the honeycomb, using wax from their own bodies. Notice that the honeycomb is made of many tiny sections called "cells." Each of the cells has six sides. This is a good shape, because cells with six sides fit together better than round cells would. Everything in God's world of nature is well planned, just like the cells in the honeycomb.

While some of the bees are busy making the comb, others fly out to find food. The bees know which kinds of flowers have the best nectar. Nectar is a sweet liquid in the flowers that is made into honey by the bees. They crawl down inside the blossoms to suck out the nectar.

A bee's tongue is long and thin so that the bee can reach into the lower part of flowers where the nectar is. The tongue is hollow, like a straw. The bee can suck the nectar through its hollow tongue into its body, just as you suck your milk through a straw.

While the bee is flying back to the hive, the nectar is mixing with another liquid inside her body to make honey. When she reaches the hive, she puts the honey into the cells of the honeycomb. Other bees fan the honey with their wings to make it thick. Still other bees put a little wax cap on the end of each cell to keep the honey from dripping out. Isn't it amazing how each bee has her own job to do and knows how to do it!

The honey is stored in the comb until it is needed as food for the baby bees or as food for all the bees during the winter when they can't get nectar from flowers.

So you see that bees need flowers. But did you know that flowers need bees? Inside most flowers is a powder called pollen. When a bee crawls into a flower to get nectar, some of the pollen from the flower sticks to the hairs on the bee's body. When she flies to another flower to get more nectar, some of the pollen from the first flower brushes off the bee into the second flower. This is part of God's plan. Most blossoms need pollen from other blossoms. Without pollen, seeds would not develop and there would not be any new flowers the next summer.

The bees need the flowers and the flowers need the bees. That's the way it is in God's world. Every plant and every animal is good for something. Animals need other animals and plants. And each plant needs other plants and animals.

Rowena Roberts

Growing

While holding a tape measure in the closed palm of my hand, I asked the children to guess what I had hidden in my hand. "What I have is eight feet long. It is shiny. It is made of steel." Upon revealing the tape measure, I measured the height of at least some of the children.

"A tape measure is for measuring. It can tell us how tall you are and how much you have grown since you were last measured. Growth is a gift of God. It is God's plan that all living things grow and change, but our height is only one way we grow. Some of the ways we grow cannot be measured with a tape measure or a scale. Can you think of any of these other ways we grow?" (Settle fights without hitting, being patient with a younger sibling or an older person, learning at school, loving and helping people who are hard to love, feeling closer to God, etc.)

"The Bible tells us very little about the boy Jesus; but one thing it does tell us is that Jesus grew to be strong and wise and that he was loved by God and people (Luke 2:52).

"A poet expressed her thanks for growing in these words. Will you make them your thanks, too, and say them after I do?" (Children repeat each line.)

> Glad I am to live!
> Glad I am to grow!
> I would grow as Jesus grew,
> Strong in body,
> Strong to do what is right and brave and true.
> Glad I am to grow! *

Adapted from material contributed by Richard Maxwell.

*Elizabeth McE. Shields, "Glad I Am to Live," *Songs and Hymns for Primary Children* (Philadelphia: The Westminster Press, 1946). Words copyright, 1946 by The Westminster Press; renewed, 1974. Used by permission.

Using a Word

The Word "Why"

Teachable element: God has planned for us to grow in learning how to take care of ourselves.

Getting started: "Why" is a word all of us use every day. No matter how old we are, we keep asking "why?". How many of you have asked:

Why do I have to eat vegetables I don't like?

Why do I have to wear boots when it rains?

Why can't I stay up and see that special movie on television?

Why did I have to fall off my bike and hurt my leg?

Conversation leads: What "why" questions do you have? What makes us ask "why"?

Pulling the lesson together: Asking "why" is a good thing. We don't always *know* why we have to do things in a certain way or why things happen. We do know that God has made us with minds to wonder and ask why things happen in a certain way. God has planned for us to grow in knowing how to take care of ourselves.

Arline J. Ban

Using an Idea

The Wonderful Human Brain

(Show a picture or a model of a human brain.)

This is a picture (or model) of a very important part of the body. It is called the brain. It is inside our head, so we don't see it; but this is what it looks like. How many parts does the brain have? Yes, there are two parts, called the left brain and the right brain. Each side has its own special work to do for us.

Put your left hand on the left side of your head for a moment. The left brain likes words and numbers. It likes to figure things out and to make decisions and memorize. Where would you need to use the left brain? (School.)

Now put your right hand on the right side of your head. The right brain understands messages without words; it gets ideas and hunches; it has feelings; it is creative. It is with this part of the brain that we worship God.

Sometimes if we let it, the left brain takes over and makes it hard for us to forget about words and decisions and problems and to let the right brain have its turn.

We invite the adults to join us as we try right now to give our right brains a chance. Look at something beautiful in this room (or close your eyes) and let the music (organ or other instrument, live or recorded) flow through you. (Listen to a brief selection, such as parts of "The Pachelbel Canon" or "Jesu, Joy of Man's Desiring" or whatever music your church considers beautiful.)

Nancy Hopkins

Hurts

Have you ever been hurt? How? (Give several children a chance to respond briefly.) Yes, there are many kinds of hurts—cuts, headaches, pains (summarize what the children have mentioned). These hurts can usually be cared for with Band-Aids or pills.

But there are some other hurts that medicine or bandages will not help. The hurts I am thinking about are different from the hurts we have just talked about. These other hurts are felt deep inside us because of unkind, mean, "put-down" words—words like "hate," "dumb," "scaredy-cat," and "sissy." These hurts are also caused by unkind actions, such as not being friendly to someone because he or she is different in some way—because of a difference in the color of skin, the kind of clothes worn, how much money the other person has, a handicap of some kind, being too little or too big. Have you ever been hurt by things like this? Would anyone care to tell us about a time you have had this kind of a hurt? (Give a few children a chance to respond briefly.)

Jesus said something important about this. He said we are not to hurt people by calling them "good-for-nothing" or "no good." He wanted to end the hurts caused by sharp, mean words.

Instead of calling people unkind names, or not being friendly, Jesus said that when we have a problem with someone, we should go to that person and work out the problem. I wonder what that would mean. What would we have to do? (Ask for forgiveness from someone we have hurt, forgive someone who has hurt us, stop using the unkind words, go out of our way to be friendly to the person, etc.)

We can help to heal the hurts of other people. Let's do it!

Prayer: Help us to be strong and brave to help others—to pick them up when they fall, to bring the medicine of love and forgiveness when their feelings have been hurt. Amen.

Adapted from material contributed by William Sutterlin.

Topical Index

Biblical Index